Edward Young Cox

The Art of Garnishing Churches at Christmas and Other Festivals

Edward Young Cox

The Art of Garnishing Churches at Christmas and Other Festivals

ISBN/EAN: 9783337379513

Printed in Europe, USA, Canada, Australia, Japan

Cover: Foto ©Thomas Meinert / pixelio.de

More available books at **www.hansebooks.com**

THE ART

OF

GARNISHING CHURCHES

AT CHRISTMAS

AND OTHER FESTIVALS.

BY

EDWARD YOUNG COX.

WITH

ILLUSTRATIONS FROM ORIGINAL DESIGNS AND ANCIENT EXAMPLES.

"All ye green things upon the earth, bless ye the Lord: Praise Him, and magnify Him for ever."—*Benedicite.*

"And a very great multitude spread their garments in the way; others cut down branches from the trees, and strawed them in the way. And the multitudes that went before, and that followed, cried, saying, Hosanna to the Son of David."—*S. Matt.* xxi. 8.

THIRD EDITION,

REVISED AND AUGMENTED BY NEW DESIGNS AND ILLUSTRATIONS.

LONDON:
COX & SONS, ECCLESIASTICAL WAREHOUSE,
28 & 29 SOUTHAMPTON STREET, STRAND.

PREFACE TO THE FIRST EDITION.

The following pages are intended to serve as a plain practical compendium of the Art of Garnishing Churches at Christmas and other Festivals. The principles of the art are briefly discussed, and the rules for applying them are given so fully that they will, it is hoped, suffice for the guidance of the most inexperienced amateurs.

The subject has been considered solely in its æsthetical aspects. A great diversity of opinion prevails as to the proper limits of Ecclesiastical Decoration; but the Author has entirely abstained from entering into that controversy. He has contented himself with giving designs and methods, varying widely in character, and suitable, some to the most elaborately, and some to the most simply, decorated edifices.

Every available treatise relating to the present and allied subjects has been considered. The information derived from these sources has been combined with the results of the Author's own practical experience—which is considerable—and with the valuable suggestions of several clergymen and others, who have successfully practised the beautiful art, which applies some of Nature's gifts to illustrate the successive seasons of the Christian year.

A grateful acknowledgment is due to several friends for the useful information contributed by them, and particularly to Mr S. J. Nicholl and Mr B. J. Talbert, for several designs which illustrate these pages.

October 1868.

PREFACE TO THE THIRD EDITION.

In issuing this, the Third Edition of "The Art of Garnishing Churches at Christmas, Easter, and other Festivals," the Author gratefully acknowledges the very favourable and flattering reception that the previous Editions have received. In the present Edition many corrections and additions have been made. Most of the Illustrations in the last Edition have been withdrawn, and a larger number of New Designs, from the pencil of Mr S. J. Nicholl, have been substituted. These the Author trusts will be found to be of an improved character, and enhanced in value by a larger number of them being executed in chromo-lithography.

November 1871.

CONTENTS.

SECTION		PAGE
I.	Historical Notes,	1
II.	General Principles,	7
III.	Methods of Forming Wreaths,	12
IV.	Devices in Evergreens,	17
V.	Devices in Everlasting Flowers, Berries, and Moss,	20
VI.	Natural Flowers,	22
VII.	Texts,	23
VIII.	Emblazoned Texts,	24
IX.	List of Texts,	30
X.	Illuminated Devices,	34
XI.	Appliqué Work,	35
XII.	Illuminated Banners,	37
XIII.	Worked Banners,	38
XIV.	Straw Devices and Texts,	39
XV.	Reredos, Dossels, and Wall Diapers,	40
XVI.	Window Sills,	42
XVII.	Screens,	43
XVIII.	Pulpits and Reading Desks,	44
XIX.	Fonts,	45
XX.	Lecterns,	47
XXI.	Coronæ and Standards,	47
XXII.	Harvest Festivals,	48
XXIII.	Materials,	49
XXIV.	Description of Plates,	50
XXV.	Polychromatic Decorations,	57

THE ART OF GARNISHING CHURCHES

AT

CHRISTMAS AND OTHER FESTIVALS.

SECTION I.—HISTORICAL NOTES.

THE decoration of Churches with flowers and foliage at Christmas and other Festivals, is sanctioned by constant usage, both before and since the Reformation. There are abundant references in old writers to this custom. For example, Spenser, in his "Shepherd's Complaint," which appeared in 1579—that is, in the reign of Elizabeth,—says:

> "Youths folke now flocken in every where,
> To gather May buskets and smeling breere,
> And home they hasten the posts to dight;
> And all the Kirke pillars ere day light
> With Hawthorne buds and sweet Eglantine
> And girlonds of Roses."

In a few words he manages to give a very complete idea of the mode in which Churches were garnished with various flowers in his day. The "posts" and pillars of the sacred building were to be decked with the fragrant blossoms of the White

Thorn, with branches of Sweet Briar and garlands of Roses.

Stowe, in his "Survey of London," which was first published about twenty years later (A.D. 1598), says:—

"Against the feast of Christmas every man's house, *as also their parish Churches*, were dressed with holme, ivy, bayes, and whatsoever the season of the year afforded to be green. The conduits and standards in the streets were garnished in the same manner."

Here, again, the modern decorator may gain one or two useful hints. The quotation from old Stowe may serve to remind us that there are other available materials at Christmas besides Holly—that the Ilex or evergreen Oak, the bay, laurel, rosemary, yew, and ivy may even in mid-winter be used to give a festive appearance to GOD's house.

Perhaps one of the most striking evidences of the antiquity of the custom is the name of the evergreen shrub Holly—evidently a corruption of "Holy." In all probability the appellation is derived from the use of holly leaves and berries to adorn Churches. The practice of decking sacred edifices with green boughs and flowers existed long before the Reformation; but it is clear that the custom was not interrupted by that event. The passages above cited are taken from authors who wrote many years after the separation of the English Church from that of Rome, and after the revision of our ritual and the adoption of our present Prayer Book. Several learned writers have collected interesting extracts from churchwardens' accounts in different parts of the kingdom, showing that during the sixteenth century flowers were frequently provided at the expense of the parishioners in adorning Churches.

Numerous authorities for this custom are given in Brand's "Popular Antiquities of Great Britain," edited by Sir Henry Ellis. Of the authorities about to be cited some are taken from that work, and some have been collected by the present writer.

Bourne, in his "Antiquities of the Common People," cites the "Council of Bracara," canon 73, as forbidding Christians to deck their houses with bay leaves and green boughs; but this extended only to their doing it at the same time with the Pagans. The practice of decking the Churches at this season is still prevalent in this country. Bourne observes that, "In the south, particularly at our Universities, it is very common to deck, not only the common windows of the town, but also the chapels of the colleges with branches of laurel, which was used by the ancient Romans as the emblem of peace, joy, and victory. In the Christian sense, it may be applied to the victory gained over the powers of darkness by the coming of Christ."

Among the ancient annual disbursements of S. Mary-at-Hill, in the city of London, is the following entry:—"Holme and ivy at Christmas Eve, iiijd." In the churchwardens' accounts of S. Lawrence Parish, Reading, 1505, "It. payed to Makrell for the holy bush agayn Christmas, ijd." In similar accounts for the Parish of S. Margaret, Westminster, 1647, "Item paid for rosemarie and bayes that was stuck about the Church at Christmas, 1s. 6d."

Coles, in his "Art of Simpling," 1656, says:— "In some places setting up of holly, ivy, rosemary, bayes, yew, &c., in Churches at Christmas is still in use."

This passage, considering the date when it was written, is very remarkable. It shows that in the time of the Commonwealth, when the Puritan party was in the zenith of its power, old customs were not altogether abrogated.

In Herbert's "Country Parson" (1657, p. 56), the author tells us "Our parson takes order that the

Church be swept and kept clean without dust or cobwebs, *and at great festivals, strawed and stuck with boughs.*"

Shakespeare, writing half a century earlier, denotes the practice of strewing rushes in the highways near Churches, upon solemn festivals. The following extract is from "King Henry IV.," Part II., Act v., sc. 5 :—

"Scene V.—*A public Place near Westminster Abbey.*
"*Enter two Grooms strewing rushes.*"

"1 *Groom.* More rushes, more rushes.
"2 *Groom.* The trumpets have sounded twice.
"1 *Groom.* It will be two o'clock ere they come from the coronation : Despatch, despatch."

A writer in the "Gentleman's Magazine" for May 1811, speaking of the manner in which the inhabitants of the North Riding in Yorkshire celebrate Christmas, says :—"The windows and pews of the Churches (and also the windows of houses) are adorned with branches of holly, which remain till Good Friday."

Gay, in his "Trivia," written about 1712, describes this custom :—

"Now with bright holly all the temples strow,
With laurel green, and sacred mistletoe."

Sir Henry Ellis, in the work cited, expresses his opinion that mistletoe " was not put up in Churches but by mistake or ignorance of the sextons ; for it was the heathenish or profane plant as having been of such distinction in the Pagan rites of Druidism." But the learned author quotes a passage from Stukeley's " Medallic History of Carausius," which states that

" The custom is still preserved in the North, and was lately at York; on the Eve of Christmas day they carried mistletoe to the high altar of the cathedral."

Palm Sunday.—Newton, in "Herbal for the Bible," says, speaking of the palm :— " The common people in some countries used to deck their

Churches with the boughs and branches thereof, on the Sunday next before Easter." In the churchwarden's account for S. Mary Outwich, London, 1510-11 is the entry :—" First, paid for palme, box, floures, and cakes, iiijd." In the accounts for All Hallows Staining, "Item for box and palme on Palme Sundays ; item for gennepore for the Churche, ijd."

The decoration of Churches with palms must not be confounded with the ceremony of " bearing of palms," which were made into crosses, to be set in the doors of houses or carried in purses. This ceremony appears to have been disused shortly after the Reformation, and to have been prohibited.

Easter.—In the churchwardens' accounts for S. Mary-at-Hill, is an entry :—" Three great garlands for the crosses, of roses and lavender ; three dozen other garlands for the quire, 3s." In the churchwardens' accounts for S. Martin Outwich, London, 1525, " Paid for *brome* ageynst Easter, jd."

A writer in the " Gentleman's Magazine," July 1783, says :—" The flowers with which many Churches are ornamented on Easter day, are most probably intended as emblems of the Resurrection, having just risen again from the Earth, in which during the severity of Winter they seem to have been buried."

Whitsunday. — Collinson, in his " History of Somersetshire," speaking of the Parish of Yatton, says :—" John Lane of this parish, gent., left half an acre of ground called the 'Groves' to the poor for ever, reserving a *quantity of grass for strewing the Church on Whitsunday*." Among the ancient annual Church disbursements of S. Mary-at-Hill, London, is the following :—" Garlands, Whitsunday, iijd."

There is a sufficient chain of evidences showing the continuance of the usage during the last century. The writers in the " Gentleman's Magazine," above cited, speak in the present tense as of a still continuing practice; but during the latter part of the last century, and the earlier part of our own, the goodly usage became in a great degree obsolete. The same spirit of indifference which suffered the churchwardens to "beautify" Churches with whitewash and hideous high pews, tolerated an almost complete neglect of a most graceful and appropriate method of marking the different seasons of the Christian year. Most of us can recollect the miserable bits of holly stuck in candlesticks and all sorts of awkward places, which were in our youth considered sufficient decorations for Christmas. Easter adornments were generally unknown; they were used, however, in a few country places, for ancient traditions are apt to linger longest in the more tenacious memories of the rural population, and old national customs are often observed in remote villages long after the vicissitudes of fashion have banished them from the busier haunts of men.

At length there came a revival of the former reverence of GOD's house, and a protest against the neglect and injuries to which it had been subjected during an age of lifelessness, irreverence, and scepticism. Among the minor advantages of the renewed taste for ecclesiology, must be reckoned a return to the ancient and thoroughly English practice of decking the sanctuary with fair flowers and pleasant verdure.

There seems a singular appropriateness in this use of the productions of nature, and the beautiful form and colour of leaves and blossoms render them the most artistic materials of decoration. It is not enough, however, that they should be employed effectively and with good taste,—it is essential, moreover, that the taste should be *Church-like*. Ornaments which would be admirable in a banquet-hall or ball-room, might be, and probably would be, utterly out of place in a sacred edifice. Religious art is necessarily more severe and sober than secular art, and more restricted to conventional types and established forms. Less strictness is required with respect to merely temporary ornaments, such as we are considering, than with respect to permanent works; but even our garlands and banners must not be divested of the ecclesiastical character.

Section II.—General Principles.

There is a fundamental difficulty of principle to be considered at the very outset of our subject, before discussing in detail the various devices and ornaments. Their colour contrasts strongly with that of the walls of the edifice, and therefore we have to examine in the first place how these lines of distinctive colour are to be disposed with reference to the architecture. Until this point is settled we ought not to begin the work of adornment. Shall the green wreaths conform with the constructive lines of the building, or be disposed independently? The first and most common idea is to adopt the stonework as a guide or pattern which is to be obsequiously followed. An ordinary house-decorator has no idea of colouring beyond that of "picking" out the mouldings. But let us hear what a writer of great eminence—who has thought deeply upon the principles of mediæval art—has to say upon this point. Mr Ruskin, in his "Seven Lamps of Architecture" (Chap. iv. sect. 36), observes:—

"Our building, if it is well composed, is one thing, and is to be coloured as Nature would colour one thing,—a shell, a flower, or an animal; not as she colours groups of things. And the first broad conclusion we shall deduce from observance of natural colour in such cases, will be that it never follows form, but is arranged on an entirely separate system. What mysterious connection there may be between the shape of the spots on an animal's skin and its anatomical system, I do not know, nor even if such a connection has in anywise been traced; but to the eye the systems are entirely separate, and in many cases that of colour is accidentally variable. The stripes of a zebra do not follow the lines of its body or limbs; still less the spots of a leopard. In the plumage of birds, each feather bears a part of the pattern, which is arbitrarily carried over the body, having indeed certain graceful harmonies with the form, diminishing or enlarging in directions which sometimes follow, but also not unfrequently oppose, the directions of its muscular lines. Whatever harmonies there may be, are distinctly like those of two separate musical parts—coinciding here and there only—never discordant, but essentially different. I hold this, then, for the first great principle of architectural colour—let it be visibly independent of form. Never paint a column with vertical lines, but always cross it. Never give separate mouldings separate colours (I know this is heresy, but I never shrink from any conclusions, however contrary to human authority, to which I am led by observance of natural principles); and in sculptured ornaments do not paint the leaves or figures (I cannot help the Elgin frieze) of one colour and their ground of another, but vary both the ground and the figures with the same harmony. Notice how Nature does it in a variegated flower; not one leaf red and another white, but a point of red and a zone of white, or whatever it may be, to each. In certain places you may run your two systems closer, and here and there let them be parallel for a note or two, but see that the colours and the forms coincide only as two orders of mouldings do: the same for an instant, but each holding its own course. So single members may sometimes have single colours—as a bird's head is sometimes of one colour and its shoulders another; but in general the best place for colour is on broad surfaces, not on the points of interest in form. An animal is mottled on its breast and back, rarely on its paws or about its eyes; so put your variegation boldly on the flat wall and broad shaft, but be shy of it in the capital and moulding; in all cases it is a safe rule to simplify colour when form is rich, and *vice versa;* and I think it would be well in general to carve all capitals and graceful ornaments in white marble, and so leave them."

In a note to this admirable passage, Mr Ruskin adds—

"It should be observed, however, that any pattern which gives opponent lines in its parts, may be arranged in lines parallel with the main structure. Thus rows of diamonds, like spots on a snake's back, or the bones in a sturgeon, are exquisitely applied both to vertical and spiral columns."

The principles of colouring architecture apply in a great degree to the subject which we are now considering, and therefore if we accept Mr Ruskin's reasoning and authority, it follows that the Church decorator is not compelled to follow with absolute fidelity the architectural lines of the building. It will be observed that Mr Ruskin himself does not assert that he is never to follow them. Indeed, in some cases the mouldings and other parts of the structure afford the most convenient means of support, and suggest the most obviously appropriate arrangements of the temporary ornaments. The forms and proportions of different Churches vary so much, that it is impossible to lay down any inflexible rule under this head. But at all events it should be clearly understood that no solecism or violation of the principles of good taste is committed by adopting lines which cross those of the architecture: and that on the contrary a servile imitation and observance of structural arrangements will produce a tame, unsatisfactory result.

A flexible wreath hanging freely suspended from two points assumes, by its own weight, the curve which mathematicians call the *catenary*. It is one of the most beautiful curves in nature, as any one will acknowledge who has observed the graceful droop of the chains of a suspension-bridge, or, on a smaller scale, of a cord hanging between two points, and not *taut*. The catenary is capable also of great variety. The droop may be very small compared with the horizontal span, so that the curve is flat and open : or, on the other hand, it may hang down so as to present the form of a narrow pendent loop. Again, a great variety of effects may be produced by using *parts* only of catenaries, and having one end of the curve considerably lower than the other. A person who possesses a moderate amount of taste and invention can contrive an endless variety of combinations in which pendent wreaths can be applied for the adornment of Churches. A great recommendation of this method is, that it is inexpensively and easily applied. When the wreath (the preparation of which we shall have to describe more particularly hereafter) is ready, all that remains to be done is to hang it over the points of suspension. No framework is needed, and the form naturally assumed is one which art would not improve.

Perhaps one of the very simplest and most easily constructed kinds of decorations is a horizontal series of plain and equal festoons: this may be continued all round the Nave, either above the windows of the aisles, or the interior arches—or both.

There does not seem to be any objection to carrying the festoons right across a window if their general level is higher than the bottom of the window. The contrast of the greenery against the glass is by no means unpleasing.

Another form of festoons slightly more complicated is that of a double series intersecting each other as in the annexed diagram.

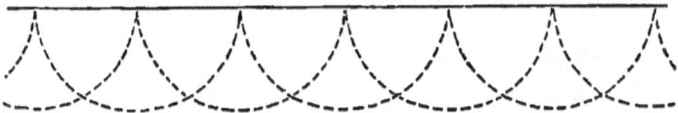

Another variation of the same idea consists of a double series of festoons one under the other; the summits of the lower series of curves being coinci-

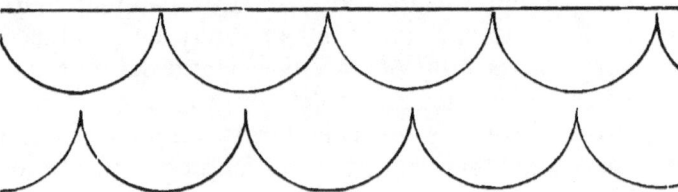

dent with the lowest points of the upper series. But in order to avoid distortion of the curves of the higher set, the lower festoons must not be suspended from them, but must have independent points of support.

Again, the catenary may be effectively employed for adorning the arcade of the nave by very large festoons hanging across the arches in the position shown by the illustration on plate 3, as the form of the wreath will appear to great advantage where it crosses the open space below the arches. An endless variety of similar devices might be suggested, and some will be found indicated by the designs in this book; but the varying circumstances and form of each Church will generally render it necessary that the decorator should be guided to a considerable extent by his own powers of invention.

The decorations should follow to a certain extent the style of the Church; thus, in a Norman building the wreaths should be massive and the round arch used. An effective arcade may be formed by a series of round arches intersecting each other.

In Early Pointed Churches the decorations would necessarily be of a lighter character, and the floral ornaments of a more refined and elegant style, and the pointed arch will of course supersede the round one.

Before entering upon details, it is advisable to suggest the desirability of making all the arrangements in good time, and for this purpose a meeting of those interested in the decorations should be called a month or six weeks before Christmas, to arrange a definite scheme on which to proceed; and if possible, a leader should be appointed, whose opinion should be final on all matters of detail.

It is also desirable to give members of the congregation the opportunity of contributing towards the decorations. This can be done either by a notice saying to whom contributions may be sent, or by having a box fixed to receive them.

Nothing is more distressing than to see those who are giving up time and attention to adorn their Church for the coming festival disagreeing on little matters of detail, and introducing an angry spirit where there should be harmony. If all understood that their individual opinions must give way to the decision of the person whom they had chosen as umpire, this element of discord could be quite avoided.

As soon as the general plan and details have been decided upon, whatever devices, banners, texts, or other materials are required, should be ordered from the professional decorator, so as to prevent the possibility of delay occurring.

Section III.—Methods of Forming Wreaths.

In all Churches, whether more or less elaborately decorated, wreaths are the staple garniture; therefore a few hints on the various ways in which they may be arranged, and the mode of constructing them, will no doubt be acceptable. Large boughs, to cut which would injure the trees, are not required; only small pieces, such as the gardeners when trimming would throw away, are wanted, as these only can be used to produce the effect desired. Almost all evergreens are suitable; but holly, by custom and by its association, should be extensively used at Christmas and all other winter festivals; as the lovely white hawthorn should be used on the feast day of SS. Philip and James, or other spring festivals of public Christian rejoicing.

The more usual plan is to fasten the evergreens with twine to a thin rope; and the most convenient and expeditious plan to adopt is, before commencing operations, to have the rope of the necessary length, stretched across the room at a convenient height (say rather more than 3 feet from the floor), and to have a quantity of evergreen sprigs assorted in heaps of different kinds, also a supply of small bunches of holly berries, and (if it is intended to use them) of everlasting flowers, arranged on a table close at hand. Begin by disposing a few of the sprigs round the rope, and fasten them on with twine; arrange the next bunch so that the stalks may not be seen, and twist the string round them, tying a knot to prevent its slipping away. This should be continued until the rope is covered; and care should be taken to use, as far as possible, a variety of tints of green, interspersed with bunches of holly berries and everlastings, as also to keep the thickness of the wreath uniform. The bunches of holly berries, if large, may be divided by splitting them through the stalks. It is desirable to wear gloves to protect the hands when making holly wreaths.

There is one objection to the use of twine for fastening the evergreens to the rope in the way described above, viz., that unless it is frequently looped or tied, as well as wound round the twigs of which the wreath is formed, they are apt to get disarranged in moving and fixing, by the twine slipping. This can be avoided by using either fine iron or copper wire in lieu of twine; the wire will bend with the wreaths, and consequently not allow the evergreens to get misplaced.

Another plan is to make the wreaths flat instead of round; the best way of accomplishing this is to use a stout string or whipcord, instead of a rope foundation—to have twigs cut with rather longer stalks than usual, and to fasten them with wire in the way described in the previous paragraph; but arranging the various pieces spreading out instead of bound close to the string; when arranged in this way, care should be taken that the choicest pieces are placed so as to show well on the face of this flat wreath.

A wreath made in this manner is more pliable, and consequently, for some parts of the work, more easily arranged than when so thick a foundation as rope is used; but it must not be forgotten that massive pillars require much thicker wreaths than those of lighter proportions; and care must be taken that all the leaves, &c., are directed upwards. This is a point that should be constantly kept in mind, as frequent mistakes are made in the matter.

Since the first edition of this work was published, an amateur who has had great experience in Church decorations has kindly favoured the author with a description of the method which he employs for wreath-making, and with some specimens.

This gentleman considers that it is far preferable to use a stout wire as the ground whereon to fasten the wreath, and fine brass wire for binding on the foliage, &c. He uses the wire over his knees, having the uncovered part on the left side and the completed work falling to the right. In this way as much as 100 feet may be made in a length, and the everlastings, or anything else that may be wished to be interwoven with the wreath, can be inserted as the work progresses. In this manner wreaths can be made either very fine, such as a single spray of box, or very thick, according to the purpose for which it is required.

The following plan of constructing the wreaths will perhaps be found to be more easily worked by ladies than either of the foregoing, and quite as effective. Instead of the wire or cord groundwork, procure some green worsted binding, and stretch it tight across a dining-room or other table, and then sew thereon the twigs, flowers, and berries, arranged in the same way as previously described. This will give a rather broad and flat wreath, which will look very well, particularly when used for decorating large columns.

Wire ribbon, *i.e.*, a wire foundation, covered with cotton, can be procured, either black or white, and this makes a capital foundation for wreaths, as the leaves can be sewn on in the same way as on to worsted binding.

For wreaths to fit into the carved moulding in the manner frequently adopted with a pleasing effect in Churches, where there is a row of arches between the nave and aisle, the best groundwork is a thin wooden lath, which, if cut to the exact length required, will, when decorated and put into its position, simply require a fastening at each end, and the natural spring of the wood will keep it in its place. A thin iron rod treated in the same manner can be bent to the required shape, and would answer equally well. In fixing wreaths, and in fact all temporary decorations, it is of the greatest importance to use as few nails or tacks as possible, and where used they should be put in with the greatest care, as it is most unsightly, and reflects discredit on the decorators, when the decorations are taken down, if the stone-work, plaster, or brick-work is found to be disfigured. In many positions a thin wire hook or staple, such as used by bell-hangers, can be driven into the joints between the stone without doing any damage, and these will often be found to be convenient for fixing the wreaths or devices.

It is a good plan to leave a few nails, staples, or whatever is used for fixing the decorations, in places where they are always required when the building is decorated, as if small and at a height from the ground they would not be observed. For wreaths round the capitals of columns, it is found to be a good plan to use a band of hoop iron with a hole punched in each end. This forms the groundwork for the wreath, and is bent to encircle the column. The ends are then fastened by a piece of string or wire. A better plan is to have the hoop iron, above described, fastened in the centre of a band of perforated zinc about three inches wide. This will enable a breadth to be given to the wreath which its position requires. Where there is a projecting moulding on which this band can rest, no other fastening is required, but where this is not the case it is better to have a hole punched in the centre of the hoop iron as well as at the ends, so that it can be fastened on each side by a piece of string, which should be tied round the column.

The authoress of "Church Floral Decorations" suggests pasting the leaves on woodwork, where the carving is delicate, as it can be easily washed off. The author of this work cannot but caution amateurs against trying any such experiment. The washing delicate wood-carving alone would be very injurious. Too great care cannot be taken to avoid doing anything that will damage either the building or its decorations.

In speaking of the construction of wreaths, allusion has been made to the use of everlasting flowers. Those who have not seen the effect of sprigs of the ordinary yellow everlasting flowers (*gnaphaliums*) introduced here and there among the wreaths in the same way as the red holly berries, will be surprised at the pleasing effect produced. The most convenient plan of introducing these is to take about three sprigs at a time, and cut off the long stalks, and bind them together with a piece of iron wire. If numbers of these tiny bunches are thus prepared, they can either be put in as the wreaths are made up, or they can be introduced afterwards in the points where they would be most effective. They could also be added, where desirable, to those wreaths which have already been fixed. The better plan, however, is to fix them in the wreath as the work progresses.

Red and other coloured everlasting flowers may be used for the same purpose. For a list of the various colours in which these flowers can be procured, see Section V.

In wreaths of ivy a striking effect is sometimes obtained by introducing a number of berries, which have first been wetted and then dipped in powdered chalk or flour.

Several designs, accompanied by full descriptions, showing the way in which wreaths can be applied to columns, arches, walls, &c., will be found on plates 2 and 3.

Here it is desirable to suggest, that as the wreaths and devices in evergreens take some days in preparation, it will be the best, as they are completed, to lay them on a stone floor, if possible, and occasionally to *slightly* sprinkle them with water. They will then be quite fresh-looking when fixed in their places.

Section IV.—Devices in Evergreens.

For forming devices, either entirely of evergreens, or of evergreens with the addition of a few everlasting flowers, perforated zinc is decidedly the best groundwork. The plan to be adopted for fixing them is as follows :—First procure the materials required, viz., the devices proposed to be decorated, cut out in perforated zinc, a supply of evergreen leaves, and very small sprays of evergreens, some stout needles, and strong thread of a dark colour— that used for sewing carpets would answer very well, or ordinary black thread would do. Some amateurs bind over the edges of the perforated zinc, or cover its whole surface with calico, to protect the hands, but, with care, this is hardly requisite.

Commence sewing on the leaves and sprays at the bottom of the device, taking care that the thread fastens the leaf down across one of the veins, and that the stalks are as far as possible covered by other leaves. For devices that are intended to be fixed at a slight elevation, small leaves should be used, and the work should be done as neatly as possible; but for those that are to be fixed at a considerable height, larger leaves would be equally, and, in some instances, more effective. Devices consisting entirely of evergreens have a somewhat heavy appearance, which is greatly relieved by small bunches either of natural or imitation holly berries, and by the yellow or other coloured everlasting flowers being introduced in different parts of the design, in the way indicated on some of the illustrations in this book, and described in the next Section.

Those amateurs who have a knowledge of drawing will find it best to make a sketch of the device in the first instance, and then with a little colour to ascertain in what position it will be best to introduce the flowers. Very effective devices can be formed by having the centre illuminated in colours, and the outer part formed in evergreens. The designs

Nos. 537 to 540 on plate 16, are intended to be worked in this way.

Another plan for forming the devices in evergreens is to have a groundwork of stout iron wire, which is of course less expensive. The leaves could be either tied on with thread, or, what is better, bound on with the fine wire used by artificial flower makers. The wire groundwork, however, is not so good as the perforated zinc, as the same breadth is not given to the design, and the leaves cannot be arranged so well, except in the case of very large devices, where the leaves could be attached by the stalks to the wire frame in such a way as to spread out.

Where devices are fixed against a window it will be requisite to stop all light passing through them, as, if this is not done, their effect would be considerably diminished. As good a manner as any of doing this is, after the device is finished, to fasten behind it some waterproofed paper, which can be procured at 2d. per yard, and being coated with the black waterproof preparation, is impervious to light.

A variety of designs are given at the end of this book for devices of various sorts. For Christmas decorations the use of the plain Latin Cross should be avoided, as the symbol of our Lord's Passion is not appropriate to this joyous season of the year. It is desirable, therefore, that whatever crosses are then used should be somewhat of a floriated character.

A large anchor, worked in box leaves, forms an effective device for any lofty position, such as the space above the chancel arch looking west.

Section V.—Devices in Everlasting Flowers, Berries, and Moss.

For working with the everlasting flowers (*gnaphaliums*), most amateurs prefer a groundwork of perforated zinc cut out to the required shape, as the stalks can be put through the holes, and fastened behind either with cotton, or by pasting or glueing stout brown paper over the back. Another plan is to have the groundwork shaped out of cardboard or of a thin piece of wood, which should be either covered with paper, or painted, and on this the flowers, cut from the stalks, are fastened down either with glue, very thick gum, or shoemakers' paste.

Melted gelatine will be found more useful than gum arabic for fixing the flowers and berries. The gelatine can be spread over the device, and the flowers laid on; but for berries it is best to dip them in a saucer containing the gelatine.

Supposing the amateur to adopt either of the above plans, he should procure the device selected, cut out to the required size, and then lay it down on a piece of plain paper, and with a pencil trace the shape. Then remove the zinc, and with watercolours try the effect of the various shades it is proposed to use; for he should always bear in mind that it is *not* requisite to adhere to one colour only with these flower decorations. Thus, a star, instead of being all yellow, could have the principal part yellow, with a green centre, and a line of red round the outside edge.

A double triangle could have one triangle yellow, edged with red, and the other white, edged with blue. The designs given on plate 23 indicate this arrangement.

By trying the effect on paper in the way suggested, the decorator is much more likely to get a satisfactory result, and it will also save time in arranging the flowers, which should be fixed in the way indicated above.

The *gnaphaliums* can be procured in the following colours:—

Yellow,	Orange or Light Red,
White,	Black,
Green,	Spotted Red,
Spotted Yellow,	Blue,
Crimson,	Violet,
Lilac,	Purple,
Pink,	Magenta,
Solferino,	

as well as some others. It should be remembered that they are real flowers dried, not artificial, as some people erroneously imagine.

The larger varieties of everlasting flowers (*helichrysum*) are grown in several colours, and these are occasionally used in conjunction with the *gnaphaliums* with very good effect, but are not so suitable used alone.

The devices when completed could have a border of evergreens surrounding them, and, if preferred, be placed on a groundwork of moss.

Letters for texts cut out in perforated zinc, wood, or cardboard, can be treated in the same way as devices. Pattern alphabets will be found on plates 13 and 14. A variety of designs covered with flowers are given on plate 23.

Many of the other designs shewn in this book are available for the same purpose, and it should be borne in mind that the perforated zinc or other groundwork for these devices will be serviceable from year to year, and that by varying their position and the arrangement of the flowers all appearance of sameness can be avoided.

Section VI.—Natural Flowers.

Where real flowers are used, arrangements must of course be made for the stalks to be kept moist, and this can very easily be done by water contained in little zinc tubes, which can be soldered in any position on to an iron frame bent to the required form; or these zinc tubes (which resemble an inverted extinguisher, and are made with a hook), can be hung on to any part of the decorations required. For flower vases, a useful frame is made in zinc which enables the decorator to make an effective bouquet with a small supply of flowers; an illustration of this and of other useful contrivances for similar purposes will be found on plate 35. Primroses for Easter decoration can be kept very well by having the stalks stuck in wet clay.

In some positions, as for instance round the base of the font, the best plan to adopt is to have oblong boxes, either of wood or zinc, to hold the water, and to have floating on them boards perforated with holes; these can be covered with moss, and the stalks, of the flowers passed through the holes to the water.

When flowers in pots are used, a convenient and effective plan is to place them in hanging wall baskets, concealing the pots with moss.

A method of arranging natural flowers in the bowl of a font is described under the head of "Fonts."

The authoress of "Church Floral Decorations," says:—"I have adopted the plan of covering all devices in which white flowers are to be used with white cotton wool, for three reasons: first, it conceals the stalks; secondly, it can be damped, and thus preserves the flowers from withering too soon, as they otherwise would do; and thirdly, when they do fade, the device still maintains its white appearance."

Section VII.—Texts.

The 82nd Canon of 1603, among other directions, requires that there be "chosen sentences written upon the walls of the said churches in places convenient."

Appropriate texts and legends are among the most effective of festival decorations. Some caution seems necessary as to the principle on which the selection should be made. Of course the words should be brief, and should have reference to the season. But besides this, it must be always remembered that they are utterances *by* the Church, and not Divine precepts and commands addressed *to* her. This distinction is not unfrequently overlooked. The letters are to be formed and put together by human hands, thence they may appropriately contain ascriptions of praise, or words supposed to be the language of the congregation; but there is something very inappropriate in the choice of words in which the Church appears not as speaker but as hearer. For example, in connection with the Holy Communion, the words "Do this in remembrance of Me," are often selected. When it is considered that these solemn words are to be fashioned out of perishable materials by human skill, there appears a singular infelicity, and almost a lack of reverence, in such a use of the sacred text. The oldest and best examples of legends and inscriptions in Churches do not involve this mistake. They are for the most part single and simple phrases, such as the thrice repeated "*Sanctus, Sanctus, Sanctus,*" and other words meet to express faith, adoration, thanksgiving, or triumph.

Section VIII.—Emblazoned Texts.

There are various modes of forming texts for temporary decorations.

The plan usually adopted by amateurs as the simplest, is to cut the letters out in coloured paper, and gum or paste them on a groundwork of plain or different coloured paper.

In order to form the letters correctly, it is best to procure an alphabet cut out in cardboard to the required size; and by laying the letters down on the paper, and running a line round them, the proper shape will be obtained, when they can be cut out with either a knife or a pair of scissors. Letters such as 500 to 502 on plate 15, printed on paper, can also be procured; these will save a good deal of time, and insure their being of the correct shape.

When the letters have been cut out, they should be fixed on the groundwork that has been prepared for them.

In order that texts may look well, it is absolutely essential that all the letters should be upright and properly spaced out; and in order to insure this, the material on which the letters are to be fixed should be arranged on a long bench or table—a dining-room table fully extended answers well; or where the work is done in the schoolroom, the school desks would be available for the purpose.

The letters should all be laid out in their proper places before any of them are fastened down. It is a good plan to rule a few pencil lines at the top and bottom of the letters, and in fixing them, to insure their being upright, either to use a T or set square, or what will answer as well, a square piece of cardboard laid on the pencil line, so that its edge will give a right angle. The necessity of keeping the letters both upright and equidistant must be strongly urged. It frequently occurs that decorations, which have evidently cost much time and attention, are completely spoiled by want of regularity.

After the letters have been fixed on the groundwork, they should be surrounded by a border; this may be made either of evergreens, with everlasting flowers introduced in the manner described on another page, or the text could be first surrounded with a border cut out of coloured papers, in one of the ways described below, and then may have an outer border of evergreens, &c., beyond the coloured one.

To make the simplest border, a narrow slip of paper, of a colour different from those used for the text, should be put round the lettering, with a cross, quatrefoil, or other ornament in each of the four corners. Thus, supposing the groundwork of the text to be plain white paper, the letters should be black with red capitals, and the border might be blue with the corners red.

If a more effective border than that produced by the simple line and corner is required, a zigzag border may be cut out in one colour with a line of a different colour on each side of it; and on this principle many other borders can be prepared.

Another plan is to procure borders painted on strips of buckram calico; these can be used for the same purpose, and admit of a great variety of designs being used.

Where paper texts, as above described, are not considered sufficiently rich in appearance, the following more elaborate plan is suggested.

Procure some white glazed buckram calico, and cut it to the required size (if fastened on a board, so much the better), then take pieces of coloured cloth, or what is better, cotton velvet, of the colour preferred, and cut the letters and borders from them in the same manner as directed for paper texts, then paste or glue them to the calico or other groundwork, surrounding the whole with borders prepared in the manner indicated above. The embroidery paste, a receipt for which is given in Section X., is the best material to use for the purpose.

The ingenuity of the decorator will doubtless suggest various other materials both for the groundwork and the letters and borders.

Very effective texts may be prepared by covering a board with green leaves, and then forming letters upon them in white cotton wool. Great care, however, must be taken, if this plan is adopted, to get the letters quite even, as, owing to the nature of the materials, it is somewhat difficult.

Another way is to prepare the board with evergreens as above described, and form the text with paper roses or camellias, which can be procured in both red and white, so that the principal letters might be red, with the remainder white, in the same manner that red and black is used in illuminating decorations in oil colours. But the propriety of using artificial flowers in Churches is somewhat doubtful.

A plan frequently adopted is to cover cardboard letters with evergreens, and fasten them to the wall separately; but the objection to this plan is, that there is a great risk of defacing the stone-work or plaster by the number of tacks or nails that would have to be used in fixing. The better plan is to use a board that has been covered with white paper, and then, when the letters have been put on, to surround the whole with a narrow border consisting of small sprigs of box or other evergreens, of which the leaves are quite small. The advantage obtained by this plan is, that the board can then be suspended in the required position upon two nails, which, besides avoiding the risk of injury to the walls above alluded to, also saves a great deal of time and trouble in fixing.

The various methods above described for making texts are all applications of the principle of cutting out one material and laying it on another; but where the decorators call in the aid of painting, a much larger field is open to them, as that art admits of a much greater variety of treatment, both as regards design and colours.

For amateurs who have not had much previous experience in illuminated decorations, it is best to procure pots of colours already prepared for use, which can be thinned with a little turpentine if found to be too thick.

The best groundwork for these decorations is " prepared cloth," a material which is painted and prepared for decoration in the same way as canvas for oil painting.

Decorations done on prepared cloth, if carefully rolled round wooden rollers before they are put away, will last for years.

When a cheaper material is required, white glazed buckram calico can be used, the process of painting being the same as on the prepared cloth.

For long texts, unless the decorators have plenty of time, it would be advisable to procure the prepared cloth and calico with the borders already stencilled, as the lengths are sold at very moderate prices.

When the material on which the text is to be written has been extended on a board or table, and the text has been spaced out, so as to obtain the proper distances between each word, the cardboard letter previously described should be laid upon it, and marked out with a black-lead pencil, care being taken to get a clear and distinct outline, and to keep the letters regular.

This being done, the next process is to fill in all the letters with their proper colours, using a camel hair, or sable brush, and putting only enough paint to cover the groundwork. When red capitals are introduced, their appearance is very much improved by running a line of black round each. Should any of the letters or ornament be required to be gilt, the leaf gold is the best to be used, and the most durable. It is sold in books, and in order to apply it properly, a gilder's cushion, knife, and brush are required, as well as gold size. The gold size should be laid on the parts to be gilt, and when it is partially dry, but still "sticky," lay out a leaf of gold on the cushion and cut it with the knife to the required size. This should be taken up with the gilder's brush and applied, care being taken that the parts are well covered with the leaf; then rub them gently over with a piece of cotton wool to remove all superfluous gold. An outline of black or red round the gold greatly improves the appearance of the gilded letters or ornament.

If the texts are not intended to be kept from year to year, and gold leaf is considered either too expensive or too troublesome to be used, bronze powder can be substituted. The work should be prepared with gold size in the way before described, and the powder, which will only adhere to the parts sized may then be dusted on.

Where gold leaf is used a nice effect is produced by having a shaped patch at the commencement of the text on which to place its initial letter, and the introduction of some fine lines of ornament in the style adopted in the old illuminated missals, will still further enrich it. See Nos. 819 to 824, plate 39.

A new material for decoration has been introduced during the last two or three years, called crystal frost. This is made of crystal glass, which, in its molten state, possesses great ductility. When in this state it is blown into exceedingly thin globules, which immediately burst and produce the frost. This material is very popular among amateur decorators.

It is used in a variety of decorations, and will adhere, without any preparation, to silk, paper, &c. The best way of applying it, however, is to use a little clear liquid gum ; but the smallest possible quantity of gum should be used, and the crystal frost not applied till it is nearly dry, only just sticky.

Letters or devices cut in cardboard or paper, and covered with the crystal frost, if placed on a dark coloured groundwork of either cotton velvet, cloth, or calico, are very brilliant.

Letters formed of everlasting flowers can be made so as to produce a most beautiful effect, as the number of colours available gives the decorator the opportunity of arranging them in a variety of ways, and several colours can be introduced in each letter. Thus in a text formed of six-inch letters, the majority of them may be formed of the yellow flowers, with a line of red running round each ; and the principal letters can be formed of white, outlined with blue ; or if larger letters are used, three or more colours could be introduced into each.

Pattern alphabets for texts, and designs for their arrangement, will be found in the illustrations, and a list of texts suitable for the various festivlas is given in the next Section.

Section IX.—List of Texts.

The following is a selection of texts suitable for festivals, and arranged in the order of the principal events of the Christian year :—

Texts for Advent.

"He cometh to judge the Earth." *Ps.* xcvi. 13.
"Behold, a King shall reign." *Isa.* xxxii. 1.
"Prepare ye the way of the Lord." *Isa.* xl. 3.
"Behold, thy King cometh unto thee." *Zech.* ix. 9.
"Hosanna to the Son of David." *S. Matt.* xxi. 9.
"Blessed is He that cometh in the name of the Lord." *S. Mark.* xi. 9.
"Watch and pray." *S. Matt.* xxvi. 41.
"The night is far spent, the day is at hand." *Rom.* xiii. 12.
"The Lord is at hand." *Phil.* iv. 5.
"Behold, He cometh with clouds; and every eye shall see Him." *Rev.* i. 7.
"Come, Lord Jesus." *Rev.* xxii. 20.
"He shall come again in His glorious majesty, to judge both the quick and the dead." *Collect for Advent.*

Texts for the Feast of Circumcision.
(*New Year's Day.*)

"His name was called Jesus !" *S. Luke* ii. 21.
"Circumcision is that of the heart." *Rom.* ii. 29.

Texts for Epiphany.

"We have seen His star in the east, and are come to worship Him." *S. Matt.* ii. 2.
"When they saw the star, they rejoiced." *S. Matt.* ii. 10.
"A Light to lighten the Gentiles." *S. Luke* ii. 32.
"They presented unto Him gifts; gold, frankincense, and myrrh." *S. Matt.* ii. 11.
"Rejoice, ye Gentiles, with His people."

Texts for Easter.

"I know that my Redeemer liveth." *Job* xix. 25.
"The Lord is King for ever and ever." *Ps.* x. 16.
"He whom God raised again saw no corruption." *Acts* xiv. 37.
"He is risen." *S. Matt.* xiv. 2.
"The Lord is risen indeed." *S. Luke* xxiv. 34.
"I am the Resurrection and the Life." *S. John* xi. 25.
"Christ was raised again for our justification." *Rom.* iv. 25.

"If we be dead with Christ, we believe that we shall also live with Him." *Rom.* vii. 8.

"Christ our Passover is sacrificed for us, therefore let us keep the feast." 1 *Cor.* v. 7.

"He is the very Paschal Lamb which was offered for us." *Communion Service.*

"Now is Christ risen from the dead, the first fruits of them that slept." 1 *Cor.* xv. 20.

"As in Adam all die, even so in Christ shall all be made alive." 1 *Cor.* xv. 22.

"O death, where is thy sting? O grave, where is thy victory." 1 *Cor.* xv. 55.

"Death is swallowed up in victory." 1 *Cor.* xv. 55.

"Thou hast ascended up on high, and hast led captivity captive." *Ps.* lxviii. 18.

"Our life is hid with Christ in God." *Col.* iii. 3.

"I am He that liveth, and was dead; and, behold, I am alive for evermore." *Rev.* i. 18.

"Alleluia! Alleluia! Alleluia!" *Rev.* xix. 1-3-4.

"Alleluia! for the Lord God omnipotent reigneth." *Rev.* xix. 6.

"This JESUS hath GOD raised up." *Acts* ii. 32.

Ascension Day.

"Thou sittest at the right hand of God." *Te Deum.*

"He ascended into Heaven." *Apostles' Creed.*

"He was taken up, and a cloud received Him out of their sight." *Acts* i. 9.

"He was received up into Heaven, and sat on the right hand of God." *S. Mark* xvi. 19.

Texts for Whitsunday.

"The Spirit beareth witness, because the Spirit is Truth." 1 *S. John* v. 6.

"The Holy Ghost, the Lord and Giver of Life." *Nicene Creed.*

"The Holy Ghost fell on all them that heard the Word." *Acts* x. 34.

"Thou only, O Christ, with the Holy Ghost, art most high in the Glory of God the Father." *Communion Service.*

"The Holy Ghost came down at this time from Heaven." *Communion Service.*

"The Comforter, which is the Holy Ghost." *S. John* xix. 26.

"Veni Creator Spiritus."

Texts for Trinity Sunday.

"The Father is God, the Son is God, and the Holy Ghost is God." *Creed of S. Athanasius.*

"Holy, Holy, Holy, Lord God Almighty, which was, and is, and is to come." *Rev.* iv. 8.

"Glory be to the Father, and to the Son, and to the Holy Ghost." *Benedicite omnia Opera.*

"Holy, blessed, and glorious Trinity, three Persons and One God."
Litany.
"God anointed Jesus of Nazareth with the Holy Ghost." *Acts* x. 38.

Texts for Harvest Thanksgiving.

"While the Earth remaineth, seed-time and harvest shall not cease." *Gen.* viii. 22.
"Man doth not live by bread alone, but by every word that proceedeth out of the mouth of the Lord." *Deut.* viii. 3.
"The Earth is the Lord's and the fulness thereof." *Ps.* xxiv. 1.
"Thou visitest the earth and blessest it, Thou makest it very plenteous." *Ps.* lxv. 9.
"Thou crownest the year with Thy goodness. *Ps.* lxv. 11.
"Praise the Lord, O my soul, and forget not all His benefits." *Ps.* ciii. 2.
"He causeth the grass to grow for the cattle, and herb for the service of man; that he may bring forth food out of the Earth, and wine that maketh glad the heart of man, and bread which strengtheneth man's heart." *Ps.* civ. 14, 15.
"The Harvest is the end of the world, and the reapers are the Angels." *S. Matt.* xiii. 39.
"He maketh peace in thy borders, and filleth thee with the finest of wheat." *Ps.* cxlvii. 14.
"Honour the Lord with thy first-fruits; so shall thy barns be filled with plenty." *Prov.* iii. 9, 10.
"The Bread of Life." *S. John* vi. 35.
"In due season we shall reap if we faint not." *Gal.* vi. 9.

Texts for School Feasts.

"The fear of the Lord is the beginning of wisdom." *Ps.* cxi. 10.
"Train up a child in the way he should go, and when he is old, he will not depart from it." *Prov.* xxii. 6.
"Remember thy Creator in the days of thy youth, while the evil days come not, nor the years draw nigh when thou shalt say, I have no pleasure in them." *Eccl.* xii. 1.
"Keep innocency, and hold fast the thing which is right, for that shall bring a man peace at the last."
"Suffer little children to come unto me; for of such is the Kingdom of God." *S. Mark* x. 14.
"Feed my lambs." *S. John* xxi. 15.
"Children, obey your parents in the Lord: for this is right." *Eph.* vi. 1.

Texts for Christmas.

"There shall come a star out of Jacob, and a Sceptre shall rise out of Israel." *Numb.* xxiv. 17.
"The right hand of the Lord bringeth mighty things to pass." *Ps.* cxviii. 15.
"The people that walked in darkness have seen a great Light." *Isa.* ix. 2.

"Unto us a Child is born, unto us a Son is given." *Isa.* ix. 6.
"His name shall be called Wonderful, Counsellor, the Mighty God, the Everlasting Father, the Prince of Peace." *Isa.* ix. 6.
"There shall come forth a Rod out of the stem of Jesse, and a Branch shall grow out of his Roots." *Isa.* xi. 1.
"The Lord, Our Righteousness." *Jer.* xxiii. 5.
"The Desire of all nations shall come." *Haggai* ii. 7.
"Behold, thy King cometh." *Zech.* ix. 9.
"The Sun of Righteousness shall arise with healing in His wings." *Mal.* iv. 2.
"Emmanuel! God with us." *S. Matt.* i. 23.
"Hosanna to the Son of David!" *S. Matt.* xxi. 9.
"Hosanna in the highest!" *S. Matt.* xxi. 9.
"The day-spring from on high hath visited us." *S. Luke* i. 78.
"Behold, I bring you glad tidings of great joy." *S. Luke* ii. 10.
"Unto you is born this day a Saviour, which is Christ the Lord." *S. Luke* ii. 11.
"Glory to God in the highest, on Earth peace, good will toward men." *S. Luke* ii. 14.
"A Light to lighten the Gentiles." *S. Luke* ii. 32.
"The Word was made flesh and dwelt among us." *S. John* i. 14.
"He came not to do His own will, but the will of Him that sent Him." *S. John* vi. 38.
"God sent forth His Son." *Gal.* iv. 4.
"God manifest in the Flesh." 1 *Tim.* iii. 16.
"We love Him because He first loved us." 1 *John* iv. 19.
"Holy, Holy, Holy, Lord God Almighty." *Rev.* iv. 8.
"Alleluia! Alleluia! Alleluia!" *Rev.* xix. 1, 3, and 4.
"Now is come Salvation and Strength." *Rev.* xii. 10.
"The root and offspring of David, and the bright and Morning Star." *Rev.* xxii. 16.
"God of God, Light of Light, Very God of Very God." *Nicene Creed.*
"God and Man is one Christ." *Creed of S. Athanasius.*
"Sanctus, Sanctus, Sanctus." *Te Deum.*
"Holy, Holy, Holy." *Te Deum.*
"Thou art the everlasting Son of the Father." *Te Deum.*
"Thou art the King of Glory; O Christ." *Te Deum.*
"Thou tookest upon Thee to deliver man." *Te Deum.*

Text suitable for Porch.

"This is none other than the House of God, and this is the gate of Heaven." *Gen.* xxviii. 17.

Texts for the Dedication of a Church.

"Glory be to Thee, O God."
"Oh pray for the peace of Jerusalem: they shall prosper that love thee." *Ps.* cxxii. 6.
"Peace be within Thy walls." *Ps.* cxxii. 7.

Section X.—Illuminated Devices.

These can be prepared in oil colours, on cardboard, calico, or prepared cloth. The device should either be procured of a professional decorator, set out ready for illumination, or a full-sized drawing should be made of it, and then traced upon the substance to be illuminated. The best way of tracing it is to prick holes all round the outline, and then lay it down on the prepared cloth or other material, and with a little whitening, tied up in a piece of muslin, dust it over. On removing the drawing it will be found that the whitening, which has passed through the pin holes, will show the outline which will enable the decorator to sketch the device easily with a black lead pencil. When this has been done, the colours and gold should be filled in in the same manner as described in Section VIII. for illuminating texts.

Most monograms and devices look best when surrounded by a wreath, composed either of evergreens or of everlasting flowers, or of the two combined.

An easy way of preparing effective devices with an illuminated centre and a flower and evergreen border, is to procure the device cut out in perforated zinc, and fix the illumination painted on prepared cloth in the centre, and then surround it with flowers or evergreens.

A simple and effective way of forming devices is to sketch out with a black lead pencil, on either prepared calico or cardboard, the outline of the monograms, crosses, or other ornaments selected, and then fill them in with a rich deep crimson in oil colour. This on the white ground, surrounded with a wreath of evergreens, interspersed with everlasting flowers and berries, will be found to have a very pleasing appearance. The monograms and crosses shown on plates 15 and 16 are suitable for this purpose.

A great variety of designs for illuminated monograms, crosses, and devices are given in the illustrations.

Section XI.—Appliqué Work.

Appliqué — of which we have no thoroughly English synonyme—is used to express the art of laying one material upon another to form a pattern, figure, or any other work that may be desired.

It will thus be seen that "appliqué work" opens a large field for the display of taste and ingenuity by the amateur decorator, more especially by the lady decorators, as it embraces work in almost every conceivable material, from coloured paper to the richest silk, velvet, or even cloth of gold. As Mulready, when asked the secret of his great success in colouring his pictures, said, "Know what you have to do," so we say, the great object of the amateur decorator should be to secure unity—*i.e.*, to make out of many things one perfect whole. And the first thing is to have the required device set out in full size ready for working, and to decide upon the materials and colours of the various parts.

To enable such of our readers as would wish to apply themselves to this appliqué work to prepare the materials selected for the purpose, we cannot do better than give the following extract from "Church Embroidery," by Mrs Dolby :—

"TO PREPARE VELVET, CLOTH, AND CLOTHS OF GOLD AND SILVER FOR APPLIQUÉ.

"Strain a piece of rather thin holland of about 1s. per yard—*not Union*—tightly in a frame, and cover it all over with 'Embroidery Paste,' carefully removing even the most minute lump from the surface. Upon this pasted holland, while wet, lay the piece of velvet or other material of which the appliqué is to be, smoothing it over the holland with a soft handkerchief, to secure its even adhesion everywhere. If there be a necessity for drying quickly, place the frame upright at a distance of four feet from the fire, holland side to the stove. But it is always best, if possible, to *prepare* the material the day before using, that it may dry naturally, the action of the fire being likely to injure some fabrics, as well as colours. The velvet, when perfectly dry, will be found tenaciously fixed to the holland, and may be removed from the frame.

"Now the entire design, or that portion of it intended to be formed of this material, is to be pounced through its pricked pattern on the holland side of the velvet, and traced correctly with a soft black lead pencil; then cut out with sharp strong nail scissors, and it will be ready for applying to the article it is designed to ornament."

The embroidery paste alluded to is made in the following manner:—Take three tablespoonfuls of flour, and as much powdered resin as will lie on a shilling; mix them smoothly with half a pint of water, pour into an iron saucepan, and stir till it boils. Let it boil five minutes; then turn it into a basin, and when quite cold it is fit for use.

If the device is intended to be worked upon velvet, cloth, or other material, the groundwork should be stretched upon a frame, and the ornaments, prepared in the way described, tacked thereon in their proper positions. This, of course, requires great care, so that the ornaments or letters may be all straight and symmetrical: for as one false note spoils the melody of a song, so one ornament or letter not properly in harmony with the others will spoil the effect of decoration. All the ornaments having been tacked on and ascertained to be in their proper places, they should be sewn on and edged with an outline of black cord; or if the ornaments should be of a dark colour, with tracing braid, either white, gold colour, or crimson and gold, as will best contrast with the work.

If, however, the device is formed of coloured

paper, all that it is necessary to do is to cut out the various parts or pieces in the desired tints, and paste them on the groundwork.

In all cases a black line should be run round the ornament, as it greatly improves the appearance of the device when placed in its position.

Much labour is almost thrown away in forming devices or texts, &c., in coloured paper, as they have always a very meagre appearance; and the same time devoted to them on painted or prepared cloth would produce work of a much more satisfactory character, and show a more advantageous return for the labour expended.

Section XII.—Illuminated Banners.

Banners can be illuminated on calico, prepared cloth, or silk. The best plan for amateurs, who have not much experience in illuminating, is to procure the materials with the ornaments set out ready for illumination from a professional decorator, and then proceed to fill in the colours in the same way as described for illuminating texts. If the ornament is not set out ready for illumination, a full sized drawing of the banner should first be made, and from it the outline traced on the material, which will then be in the same state of forwardness as if supplied by the professional decorator.

Care should be taken in arranging the ornament on banners, to leave room for the hem at the top, which should be made sufficiently large for the cross pole to pass through. The cross pole should be a rod from $\frac{1}{2}$ to $\frac{3}{4}$ of an inch in diameter, with a terminal at each end either of turned wood, painted and gilt, or a metal fleur-de-lis or cross either of iron or brass. A cord to suspend the banner should be of the two principal colours used for the banner.

Banners have a very pleasing appearance when hung on the walls between the windows in the nave or chancel; and also when there are columns and arches between the nave and the aisles they look very well if hung upon the spaces between the arches. A large loop or knot of evergreens can be fixed at the point from which the cord of the banner is suspended, or a wreath of evergreens can be hung in a festoon at the top and sides of the banner.

Section XIII.—Worked Banners.

These can be made in various ways; those embroidered by hand, when well designed, and executed by one skilled in church needlework, are of course the most beautiful, as the variety both of materials and designs at command is almost unlimited. The handsomest are those embroidered on silk, whilst cloth, bunting, or other material is available for less expensive decorations.

For temporary purposes, however, it is not often thought desirable to spend so much time or money on the banners as embroidery usually involves, so that where worked banners are adopted, they are more frequently made in appliqué work, the process of preparing which has already been fully described on page 35; thus, supposing it is proposed to make a crimson banner with a white cross or monogram surrounded with four gold stars, and having a short text such as "Alleluia," the groundwork could be of crimson cloth, the cross or monogram of gold-coloured cotton velvet, and the text of white cotton velvet; and when the ornament is fixed on the groundwork it may be edged with black or coloured cord, or tracing braid, as previously suggested; and the material then taken out of the frame, cut to the shape decided upon, and made up with a hem at the top for the cross pole to pass through, and an edging of cord or fringe.

Section XIV.—Straw Devices and Texts.

Those who have never seen decorations worked in straw have no idea how effective they are. There are several different ways in which straw can be applied to decorations. The easiest plan is to use the straw tissue which can be procured in small sheets, the letters or devices are then cut out to the required size and mounted on the groundwork with paste. A crimson cotton-velvet ground, with inscription or ornament in straw tissue letters, is very effective. Another plan is to use the straw plaits which can be procured in hanks of long lengths and various widths; but care should be taken to get a good pliable quality, as most sorts are brittle and crack or break when bent about much.

The letters or devices to be formed with these plaits should be first cut out in cardboard and then the straw sewn on to them. The straw can be applied either flat or in high relief, according to the taste or skill of the decorator.

A lady amateur recently sent the author some banners worked in high relief, with the straw in some parts turned on edge and formed into a roll, and in others sewn on, so as to give a projection of nearly an inch to the straw. The groundwork of these banners was cotton velvet on crimson, white, and other colours, and the effect of them was very good.

A third plan of working on straw is to procure

whole straws, sold in bundles, and to split them with a small tool which is made for the purpose, and with these to form the required design.

Section XV.—Reredos, Dossels, and Wall Diapers.

The east end of the church should, of course, be the part chiefly decorated. When there is a reredos, its design will determine the mode in which decoration should be applied.

Taking the general type of reredos—viz., one of either wood or stone, with panels divided by columns, it would be a good plan to carry a massive wreath of evergreens, with or without flowers, right across the string course, and to run smaller wreaths round the mouldings. The panels could then be filled with a groundwork of evergreens, and have a device worked in everlasting flowers in the centre of each. If the string course be continued to the north and south walls of the chancel, the space below it on each side of the altar table could be filled in with a wall diaper, constructed in the manner described below.

The foregoing plan is arranged upon the system more generally adopted of following the architectural lines; but the preferable course is to act on the reverse principle—viz., to hang the wreaths of foliage in festoons from point to point, in the way described at the commencement of this book, and illustrated in the photographic view of an interior, on plate 2.

By adopting this plan, the architectural mouldings are not nearly so much hidden as in the former one.

The coloured illustration on plate 9 gives a design for an effective temporary reredos; a number of other designs are also given for them in the illustrations.

Where there is no reredos (or only a very plain one, which it would not be objectionable to hide) a very pleasing effect can be obtained by constructing a temporary structure in the place of a reredos. This can be done much more easily than will at first be imagined, and a great variety of designs can be arranged with very simple and inexpensive materials. But care must be taken to avoid an infraction of the fundamental canon of church decoration—regard for truthfulness—and to give the suggested structure the distinct character of temporary ornament. All mere mimicry of permanent work ought to be scrupulously shunned.

The framework for simple designs can be made entirely of laths and stout wire; but for more elaborate patterns the framework is best made of thin round iron rods, and the devices either of iron wire or perforated zinc. A variety of simple things in ordinary use will suggest themselves to the mind of the intelligent decorator, such as using children's hoops of various sizes to form circles.

If the top of the leafy reredos is surmounted by a canopy, or if it consists of a series of canopy-shaped arches, these can be very easily crocketed by mounting two or three sprays on wire, and then the crockets so formed can be fixed by twisting the end of the wire round the arches at regular intervals.

Wall diapers for chancels, formed of evergreens and flowers, have a very pleasing effect against the east end of the chancel, either on the north and south sides of the altar table, with a temporary reredos, formed in the way described above, over it, or else covering the whole of the east wall to any height that may be convenient.

Diapers can be made either entirely of stout iron wire, or a combination of wooden laths, or strips of perforated zinc and wire. An infinite variety of designs can be arranged in this manner, from the simple lattice to the most elaborate set patterns, filled with emblems and devices.

Those of a simple character look very well if laid on a groundwork of the white buckram calico. For others, more elaborate, unglazed cotton of various colours can be used, either with or without the white, to vary the background according to the requirements of the design.

For diapers of an elaborate character the whole of the groundwork could be cut out of sheets of perforated zinc, and on this material they can be more readily worked and more easily fixed. Effective wall diapers can also be made by having the simple lattice pattern very open, covering it with evergreens, and illuminating, in oil colours or gold, small ornamental crosses and other devices on the white calico groundwork. When there is no reredos, an effective dossel can be formed, either in stuff with ornaments in appliqué, or in calico or prepared cloth, illuminated as in the designs on plate 33.

An inexpensive Christmas frontal can be made in the same way. See plates 33 and 34.

Section XVI.—Window Sills

Can be very effectively decorated by procuring a board about an inch thick, cut to the shape of the sloping sill, and having it perforated with holes all over about 2 inches apart, and sticking sprigs of evergreens into these holes, covering the board with moss. Another plan is to fit boards into all the window sills, and cover them with moss or leaves, and form a text in everlasting flowers to run all round the church. In a church where the author saw this plan adopted, the text, which was worked in white everlastings, was—

"His name shall be called Wonderful, Counsellor, the Mighty God, the Everlasting Father, the Prince of Peace"—

and the effect was very satisfactory.

Texts on the same plan can of course be formed in various ways, or, if it is preferred, a device instead of a text may be placed in the centre of each window-sill on the groundwork of leaves or moss.

The texts can also be illuminated in colours on calico, and surrounded with wreaths of evergreens.

Here it is desirable to remark that wherever damp moss or any other material likely to leave a stain on the stonework is used, it will be requisite to put waterproof paper, or something of a like nature, underneath it. For this reason the French dried moss is generally preferable for decorative purposes, and it is also a better colour.

Section XVII.—Screens.

Where there are one or more screens, either of wood or metal work, in a church, they present an opportunity for very telling decorations. Supposing the screen to be a large one, with columns supporting tracery panels and a cornice above, the most obvious way of decorating it will be to twist very slight wreaths round the columns, to run wreaths of evergreens, either with or without a text between them, along the cornice, and to introduce in the panels, monograms, crosses, and devices, either formed of berries and leaves, everlasting flowers, or painted in oil colours on a groundwork of calico, prepared cloth, or other material.

The suggestion given, under the head of "Reredosses," on the subject of hanging wreaths in festoons, will equally apply to screens.

The Rev. E. L. Cutts, in his work on "Christmas Decoration," speaking of screens, says:—

"The architectural effect of many churches would be very much improved by the restoration of a screen to the chancel arch. The Christmas decorations afford an opportunity to try the experiment by the erection of a temporary screen, which may easily be formed of a few splines, hoops, and pieces of wire covered with evergreens.

"The effect of a side screen to hide the organ, or of a screen to the tower arch to keep off the draft, where the tower is used as an entrance to the church, may be similarly tried in this temporary work."

It is, however, a matter for consideration whether it is wise to erect a temporary screen; for, apart from the argument which some might urge, that a screen constructed in the way described is "a sham," there is the weighty objection, especially in the case of one across the chancel arch, that unless very light and open, it may shut out the view of the principal decorations.

Here again the special features of the building to be decorated must be taken into consideration, in order to determine whether it is desirable to have such a temporary screen.

Section XVIII.—Pulpits and Reading Desks.

The pulpit and reading desk, being conspicuous objects, require special care and attention, and being near the congregation, and on the line of sight, whatever decorative work is applied to them should be executed in the best possible manner.

Here, as in almost all other parts, the evergreen wreaths should play an important part. They may run round the cornice, plinth, and surbase moulding; then very light and delicate ones might surround the panels, and if the pulpit is supported on columns, these also may be wreathed in the same way as the larger columns in other parts of the church.

The panels of the pulpit offer to the amateur a fine opportunity for displaying good taste in decoration. Numerous devices, suitable for the purpose, can be selected from the illustrations in this book, and they should of course be worked in a smaller size, and with more choice materials than for the wall devices. Nothing tells better for the decoration of pulpit panels than devices worked in everlasting flowers of various colours; and if the groundwork of the panels is covered with cloth or velvet before the devices are laid on, the appearance would be greatly heightened. A very effective design for decorating a pulpit with festoons is given on plate 10.

Section XIX.—Fonts.

The festival of Christmas is one at which it would seem to be peculiarly appropriate to give the font special care. All decorations, therefore, that are attempted for it should be made as effective as possible, and of the choicest materials.

An idea that has been frequently adopted of late is to form a cross of white lilies, arranged in such a manner as to float in the bowl of the font; this has a beautiful appearance, and is very appropriate. A circular board of the right size floats on the top of the bowl, perforated with holes, through which the flowers can be passed to form the cross, the remainder of the space being filled in with moss. But unless the font is lined with some impervious material, there is danger of injuring it by this treatment. A far preferable method is, to fit into the font a movable zinc basin, No. 758, plate 35 —this can be removed when the font is required for baptisms,—or a zinc trough in the shape of a cross, Nos. 754 or 756, plate 35. These permit frequent renewal of the water without disturbance to the decorations, and afford an opportunity of placing *dry* French moss round the rim. The perforated wood on which the flowers are arranged will, if this method be adopted, float within the interior basin or trough.

An iron framework, to form a temporary upright cover, four or six feet high, to a font, can be procured at a very moderate price, and this forms an excellent groundwork for a leafy decoration; or a simple frame for the same purpose can be constructed of laths and wire.

Another method of decorating a permanent upright font cover is to attach a light iron wire framework to it, from which light sprayey wreaths of foliage, arranged with great care, and of the rarest and best sorts of evergreens available, should be suspended.

Where the panels of the font are plain, or there is no objection to their being covered up, devices, either in illumination, appliqué work, or everlastlasting flowers, can be fitted in each.

Many fonts are very handsome in themselves, with rich carving and inlaid work. Where this is the case, the temporary decoration should be applied so as to heighten their beauties, and not by any means to hide them. But where the font is plain in itself, there is no objection to its being much more profusely covered with decorations, in the way suggested on plate 10.

A massive wreath of evergreens, the appearance of which would be greatly improved by the introduction of some Christmas roses, can be laid round the base of the font, and from this could spring, where the design admits of it, wreaths of foliage and flowers twining round the stem in any of the ways indicated in the designs for decorating columns given on plate 3. If the font is raised on one or more steps, these could be covered with waterproof paper to prevent discolouration, and then moss should be laid on them, which could either be left plain or enriched with texts or other devices formed in everlasting flowers, &c.

Section XX.—Lecterns.

The lectern should not be neglected by the decorator, as from the central position in which it is placed, it is in full view of the whole congregation.

The base and stem may be wreathed with evergreens and flowers, in any manner that its construction suggests; and if the lectern has a single bookboard, a device worked in everlastings may be introduced in the front part of the top; or, with a very pleasing effect, a small banner, bearing an appropriate device or text, may be suspended from the top edge of the lectern. If the device is placed sufficiently low down, the banner may cover the bookboard, and hang over the front of it, in the way indicated by the illustration on plate 10. Should the lectern be a very plain one, it could be enriched by introducing spandrils or other ornamentation, formed of stout iron wire, at the base and underneath the bookboard, as a foundation for further decoration.

Section XXI.—Coronæ and Standards.

These form good groundwork for effective decoration. For the former, a perforated zinc crown for the top, decorated with everlastings and berries, with wreaths formed of evergreens, hanging from it to the band of the corona, is recommended.

Evergreen chains may also be carried round the band, and, at intervals, shields cut out of cardboard, and decorated with the sacred monogram or some emblem, would have a good effect.

The gas standards can be treated entirely with wreaths of evergreens and everlastings, and the most effective mode of applying them is obvious—viz., to run them spirally up the stem, and hang them in festoons across the branches.

Where the church is lighted by wall brackets, they can be wreathed with foliage, and a small device or banner suspended from each.

Designs shewing a novel way of applying the wreaths to coronæ and standards will be found on plate 11.

It is hardly necessary to say that any decorations attached to the lighting arrangements of a building should be fixed in such a way as to be free from risk of catching fire, or being blackened by smoke.

Section XXII.—Harvest Festivals.

It has now become such a frequent practice to hold harvest festivals, that this work would hardly be complete without a few words on the subject.

The obvious plan to adopt at such a season is to use the fruits of the earth, as much as possible, for forming whatever decorations may be attempted, but, at the same time, to avoid those extravagances one sometimes reads of—such as standing a sheaf of wheat on each side of the altar table, or making the pulpit look like a gigantic sheaf of wheat.

Texts, either straight or curved, for arches, painted on calico or prepared cloth, can be bordered very effectively with corn, grapes, hops, or other fruit, and flowers,—scarlet geranium has a beautiful effect among the corn. Individual taste will suggest the most suitable arrangements for each building. The texts could also be on a groundwork of crimson cotton velvet, with letters in straw, such as No. 738, plate 35, the borders also worked in straw, or with fruit and corn. Other devices formed in straw are shown on the same plate, and some straw banners, and others suitable for harvest festivals, on plates 24 and 26. The addition of ears of wheat and barley, &c., would make these very appropriate for the occasion. Wall devices can also be surrounded with wreaths in the same way as the texts.

Section XXIII.—Materials.

A concise list of materials likely to be required by the amateur church decorator will possibly be of service. To commence with evergreens. Of the holly, which is by custom the principal one used, there are sixteen varieties, the common one being the *Ilex Aquifolium*.

Holly.
Variegated Holly.
Ivy (the smaller variety).
Laurel.
Box.
Yew.
Fir (in its various varieties).
Arbor Vitæ.
Portugal Laurel.

Arbutus.
Lauristinus.
Ferns.
Privet.
Myrtle.
Cypress.
Bay.
Rosemary.
Moss.

Drummond observes, speaking of January :—

"Many cryptogamous plants, especially mosses, now put on their best attire, and to the inquiring eye exhibit a structure more beautiful than is to be perceived in the noblest trees of the forest."

MATERIALS FOR FORMING WREATHS—

Evergreens, as previous list.
Everlasting flowers.
Imitation Holly berries.
Rope.
Stout string.
Fine twine.
Stout iron or copper wire.
Fine   do.   do.
Reel wire (as used by artificial flower-makers).
Needles and thread.
Hoop iron.
Deal laths.

Scissors (best tied by a long tape to wrist or waist when in use).
Pocket knife.
Pliers (for wire).
Hammer.
Nails and tacks.
Frame for decorated font cover.
Bands of perforated zinc.
Letters of do. do.
Zinc and iron clips for capitals of columns.

FOR EVERGREEN OR FLOWER DEVICES.—The groundwork cut out in perforated zinc in addition to the foregoing.

FOR WORKED AND PAINTED DEVICES.—Full sized models of monograms, crosses, and devices.—These are best procured cut out in cardboard, except where a professional decorator is employed to prepare them ready for illumination, or the amateur has sufficient knowledge of drawing and of their correct proportions to set them out himself.

Cloth (in various colours).
Cotton velvet   do.
Cotton wool.
Cartoon paper.
Coloured papers.
Coloured flock papers.
Imitation gold paper.
Imitation silver paper.
Prepared (painted) cloth.

Prepared calico.
Paints, prepared for use.
Gold leaf.
Gold size.
Paint brushes.
Straight rule.
Set square.
Compasses.*

SECTION XXIV.—DESCRIPTION OF THE PLATES.

Plate 1.

FRONTISPIECE,—

This photograph shows the interior of a large handsome church of good architectural proportions, and the design includes both its permanent and temporary decorations. The representation of the Lord's Supper above the chancel arch is in English mosaic work, or in hand-painted art tiles, and the decorations on the roof in colour; both of these are of

---

* For large circles, a nail or pin, driven in at the point from which the circle is struck, with a string of the required length, having a pencil attached to it, revolving round it, form a good substitute for compasses.

course permanent. The temporary decorations are the dossil, which is of coloured cloth bordered with lace, bearing an illuminated or embroidered text and device, with wreaths of foliage hung in festoons. The columns of the chancel arch and the wall space adjoining, have wreaths of evergreens, and the arch itself is surrounded with a text illuminated on prepared cloth, the spandrils being filled in with foliage, on which is fixed a pair of the banners, such as are shown on plates 24, 25, and 26. A text also on prepared cloth is carried round the nave under the clerestory windows; the columns to the nave arches are wreathed, and the spaces between these arches are covered with evergreens bearing devices, either illuminated or worked in everlasting flowers.

Plate 2.

This design shows the interior of a church decorated upon the principle suggested in the earlier part of the book—viz., the adoption of festoons, curved lines and diapers, instead of the more usual plan of following the architectural lines of the building only. For further remarks on this method of decoration, see Section 11.

The reredos at the end of the church is formed on a framework of iron wire, and the shields and devices are cut out in cardboard, and illuminated. In order the more clearly to show the decorations, no furniture or internal fittings are shown.

Plates 3 and 4.

Plate 3 shows a portion of the nave of a church with its arcade and clerestory. The columns are decorated by laths tied to them, so as to avoid the necessity of injuring the masonry; festoons of foliage are then to be twisted round the columns, and fastened to the laths. The arch is decorated by a lath bent to the soffit, to which natural foliage has been fixed. The clerestory being difficult to reach, it is suggested to decorate it by devices in perforated zinc covered with the everlasting flower and foliage. These, when prepared, would be easily suspended from hooks, which would remain for use from year to year. The spandrills of the arcade are enriched with banners and festoons. The walls and the aisles seen through the arches are decorated with diaper work, formed by laths and natural foliage. Plate 4 gives the details of the proposed decorations shown on plate 3 to a larger scale.

Plate 5.

The devices A, B, C, and D are for wall diapers. A is simply formed by stout wire bent to the shape shown, and secured by twisted wire at the intersections, and then covered with natural foliage, holly, or laurel, enriched, if desired, with rosettes of everlasting flowers, or with bunches of berries at the junction; the other diapers are formed by laths of different widths crossing each other, to which the foliage can be applied as individual taste may suggest.

E and F are decorations applied to a gallery front : they are constructed with laths, as before described, with devices formed in everlasting flowers, the cross star, &c., as shown on plate 23; in design F, festoons are added. Design G is a decoration for Communion railing, formed by two cords passing from one standard to another, to which narrow bands of canvass, with natural foliage and berries, are secured.

Plate 6.

In this plate, the part printed in black is supposed to be the permanent dossil wall decoration, &c.; and to this is added, printed in colours, the temporary decorations, consisting of suspended festoon, of wreaths of everlasting flowers and foliage, and on the window-sills a cross and trefoil, formed of zinc, contrived to hold water and natural flowers.

Plate 7.

In this is a design for decorating the end of the chancel entirely by temporary decorations. The curtains being made of coloured unglazed cotton, or any other suitable material, are hung on either side; on these a framework of laths is formed, adorned by natural foliage, berries, or everlasting flowers. The inscription, as well as the figures carrying our Lord's name, are to be painted on prepared cloth; the frontal would be made of cloth, the pattern formed by sewing on a cord twisted to the design shown. The cross and other finials to the dossel are of everlasting flowers.

Plate 8.

This is a second design for the decoration of the chancel, &c., by a combination of painting and floral decoration. The portions of the design printed in black and white are supposed to be the permanent portions; the dossel is of painted cloth, divided into panels by bands of natural foliage, the wreaths in the upper part being of the everlasting flowers; other devices may be submitted for the wreaths if wished. The cross is one of the zinc ones before described, filled with natural flowers; the vertical bands on either side of the dossel are next to the wall, one formed by strips of paper or cloth folded to the pattern indicated, and fitted out with natural foliage and berries; the remainder of the design is made out with squares, quatrefoils, and crosses formed of foliage, berries, and everlasting flowers sewn, or otherwise affixed, to the cloth background.

Plate 9.

This design, being printed in colours, needs little explanation. The framework should be made of laths, iron rods, wire, and perforated zinc. The blue stars should be painted on a groundwork of the buckram calico. The crowns and the A Ω might be either worked in everlasting flowers or cut out in cardboard and illuminated. The ornamental cross, and the other coloured ornament, is proposed also to be worked in flowers; but if sufficient time could not be spared to do this, with a little alteration the designs could be carried out in illuminations on calico or card surrounded with foliage, with everlasting flowers intermixed.

Plates 10 *and* 11.

In these plates a number of ideas is suggested for decorating the internal fittings of a church principally with wreaths of foliage variously treated, introducing everlasting flowers in different parts. The ornamental shields introduced in the panels of the font should be illuminated on cardboard, and the devices shown on the pulpit, the reading-desk, and the screen, should be worked in everlasting flowers, or, if wished, they also might be illuminated in oil colours. The framework of the font cover should be made of iron wire about a quarter of an inch in diameter. Other methods of decorating the various articles of church furniture will be found described under the heads of Fonts, Pulpits, Lecterns, Coronæ, &c.

Where there is no permanent font cover, or where there is only a flat one, a very effective one can be constructed of wire. See plate 35.

Plate 12.

This photograph gives a number of devices to be worked in everlastings. Owing to the great assortment of colours in which those flowers can be obtained, the variety of designs that can be produced is endless, as the same may be repeated many times treated in a different way. This is useful when a supply of perforated zinc devices has been procured, as they can be used from year to year without reproducing the same arrangement of design.

Plates 13 *and* 14.

Patterns of four different sorts of alphabets and numerals to correspond are here given. For forming texts, it is best to procure an alphabet cut out in cardboard to the required size, and with a lead pencil to trace the shapes in their proper positions; after this is done, they can be filled in with the required colours, or cut out to shapes, as the case may be.

Letters of these patterns can also be procured printed on paper, which can be cut out for use and coloured as wished.

Plates 15 and 16.

These two sheets give designs for monograms, crosses, crowns, stars, and a variety of other devices suitable for cutting out in cardboard or perforated zinc. Most of them need but little explanation, but regarding a few of them some remarks may be advisable.

With regard to the usual monogram of our Saviour's name, it is a mistake to suppose that it was intended originally to convey the meaning of *Jesus Hominum Salvator* (Jesus the Saviour of Men), as it is of Greek and not Latin origin, formed by the first three letters of our Saviour's name in Greek.

It is a much disputed point whether this monogram should be written I.H.S. or I.H.C., and there seems to be no definite authority to settle the question, for as early as the ninth and tenth centuries, coins which are in existence prove that even at that time both forms were used.

Engravings of some of these coins; of Basilius the First, A.D. 867, Constantinus VII., about 912, and Zimeces, about 969, are given in the Calendar of the Prayer-Book, published by James Parker & Co.

The letters X.P. equally represent the Saviour's name. They are the Greek initial letters of the name Christos (ΧΡΙΣΤΟΣ), and occur in the early Christian tombs at Rome, in the first and second centuries.

As regards the various forms of crosses, the Latin Cross, No. 520, is too well known to need explanation. No. 541, the Maltese Cross, has eight points, which are said to be symbolical of the eight beatitudes. No. 542 is the St Andrew's Cross. No. 543 is the Cross of Calvary. No. 544 is the Cross Crosslet, being composed of four Latin crosses; and No. 545 is the Greek Cross, which is said to represent the spread of the gospel throughout the world, as taught by the four evangelists.

Plates 17 and 18.

These plates contain a variety of monograms, crosses, and devices, suitable for illuminating in colours on a groundwork of cardboard, calico, or prepared cloth. The small designs

A, B, 572 to 575, are proposed to be illuminated on silk, and are suitable for the fall or antipendium to the bookboard of either the pulpit or the lectern. They could also be worked in everlasting flowers for the same purpose with very good effect.

Plates 21, 22, *and* 23.

The designs on plates 21 and 22, and some of those on plate 23, are intended for painted decoration. Many of them bearing texts, they are suitable for placing on the walls, between the windows of the north and south aisles of a church, or over aisle arches. No. 623 shows a narrow painted ribbon text wound round the column; it is attached by means of a cord, to prevent injury to the stone. Nos. 628 to 642 give a variety of devices suitable for working in everlasting flowers, for fixing in panels of pulpits, reredos, font, screen, &c.

Plates 24, 25, *and* 26.

These plates contain a great variety of designs for banners, suitable for illuminating on silk, prepared cloth, or calico. Nos. 674 to 676 are for working in appliqué, in the manner previously described; others could also be worked in the same manner. Nos. 677 to 679 are specially designed for working in straw. Any variation wished can be made in the texts on these banners, so as to make them suitable for other seasons than Christmas.

Plates 27, 28, 29, *and* 30.

Various designs for texts, and for borders suitable for texts, are given on these plates.

The texts, with a fall below them, as Nos. 687 to 690, have a very pleasing and beautiful effect when well executed, and are particularly suitable for the north and south sides of the chancel.

Nos. 694 to 698, it will be seen, are designs for arch texts. There is often some difficulty in taking the measurement of a large chancel archway for a text, and the designs 694 and 697 are designed so as to avoid the necessity of the sweep being taken accurately; for these not being arranged to follow the line of the arch, the exact radius is not required. Where a design such as 698 or 706 is selected, the best way to procure the measurements is to take them from A to B, B to C, and D to E. The latter dimension gives the radius with tolerable accuracy; if perfect accuracy is required, a paper mould should be taken, in addition to the figured dimensions. The small texts and scrolls are for fixing on either side of the chancel arch, or in any similar position.

Plates 31 *and* 32.

These plates, which are also for painted decorations, are principally suitable for Easter, but most of the designs would be suitable for Christmas or any other festival, if the texts were altered.

Plates 33 *and* 34.

Plate 33 gives three designs for temporary reredoses or dossels suitable for illuminating on either prepared cloth or calico. The altar frontals, shown on the same page, can also be illuminated in colours, or the designs to be cut out and worked in appliqué. The three designs on plate 34 are also intended for dossels.

Plates 35 *and* 36.

The designs 737 to 745 are for letters and devices worked in plaited straw and straw tissue. Nos. 746 and 747 are hanging baskets for flowers. The remainder of the designs on Plate 35, with the exception of the shields 760 and 761, and the font-cover frames 765 and 766, are for holding water or wet sand for cut flowers, either in flower vases, or for placing in or round the font, and in other positions. The troughs 754 to 759 are also suitable for placing on graves.

Plate 36 gives a number of designs for flower vases, both in polished brass and in china.

Plates 37, 38, *and* 39.—*Printed Devices.*

Nos. 788 to 795 are devices, about seven inches square, suitable for the panels of a font, or for fitting in behind evergreen wall diapers, &c. Nos. 796 to 803 are shields, rather less than a foot long, suitable for the panels of pulpits, reading-desks, &c., or for the centres of wall devices. Nos. 804 and 805 are also for centres of wall or panel devices; the remainder are larger devices, which would look well surrounded by wreaths of foliage in the spaces between the windows of the nave, or on each side of the chancel arch.

Section XXV.—Polychromatic Decorations.

Although the main object of this work is to aid the amateur in forming temporary decorations appropriate to the various festivals, and to suggest ideas to be executed in flowers, foliage, and other frail and perishable materials, it has been thought advisable to devote a short section to the subject of permanent polychromatic decorations.

In every age in which art has flourished, the architect, painter, and sculptor have worked hand in hand, the work of the painter being strictly decorative; not, however, losing sight of the higher teaching power of his art, by which in mediæval days he made the walls of the church the Bible history of the poor. The easel picture framed as a distinct object, the idea of which may be described as the representation of an event seen through an open window, was then unknown, and all the skill of pictorial art tended to adorn the works of the architect, and the furniture of the building.* Until the easel picture came into fashion, and isolated the painter and his work from his brother artists, every system of architecture admitted the aid of colour, intended from the commencement of the work to be applied either by the skill of the painter or by the use of the more costly mosaic. The temples of Egypt, Assyria, and Greece, and in later times the Christian churches of northern Europe, glowed in colour; and the magnificence of Byzantine and Roman art, gorgeous in gold and coloured mosaic, strike us with wonder and admiration. For the large wall spaces, the curved walls of the apse, and the domes

---

* Du jour que le tableau, la peinture isolée, faite dans l'atelier du peintre, s'est substituée á la peinture appliquée sur le mur qui doit la conserver, la decoration architectouique peinte a été perdue.
—Viollet-le-Duc.

of Byzantine and Roman art, no decoration is so magnificent or appropriate as mosaic; but for the Gothic church the metallic lustre and changing effect do not always accord with the architectural pillar, arch, and vault—the

> "Branching roofs
> Self-poised and scooped into a thousand cells,
> Where light and shade repose."

The use of mosaic should in such structures be confined to small works, monuments, or furniture, to the panels of the reredos, font, or pulpit. In such objects it is alike beautiful and enduring, and modern research has succeeded in reviving the manufacture of the golden, white, and coloured tesseræ, by which the skilled artist may rival the works of old in their beauty and durability. With reference to mosaic, we may allude to paintings in enamel, on pieces of opaque-coloured glass, especially made for this purpose, and to pictures produced on the system of the Florentine mosaic by marble inlay, assisted by incised lines. Encaustic and majolica tiles are also now made, especially designed for mural decoration, and what is far preferable, hand-painted tiles, which possess all the advantages of moulded or stamped tiles, without their mechanical effect, often inappropriate ornament, and sameness of character. These, and other means, are now at the disposal of the artist, which enable him to produce the most charming effects, worthy of the grandest buildings, without excessive expense.

Splendid, however, as the works of the mosaicest are in buildings, where every part can be equally glowing in gold and colour, it is equally interesting, and more to our purpose, to study the decorations of our northern edifices, in which effects worthy to be compared with those we have mentioned were often obtained by the use of three or four simple colours, happily contrasted with lines and spaces skilfully designed and proportioned. This is the school of art which we must study for our Gothic churches, not only because the results come within the means at our disposal, but because they serve to enhance the beauty of the architectural forms, rather than to intrude themselves upon our notice. Of colour applied to the exterior of buildings, it would be out of place to do more than allude to here; but that colour was partially so applied, we have some evidences, notwithstanding the ravages of time. It was the interior, however, of churches, halls, and rooms, that our ancestors delighted to clothe with hanging tapestry and painted decoration. Chaucer describes a room as—

> "Full well depainted,
> And al the walles with colors fine
> Were painted to the texte and glose,
> And all the Romaunte of the Rose."

The church built at Wearmouth in the seventh century[*] was so decorated, we are told, that "the most illiterate peasant could not enter the church without receiving profitable instruction;" and there is scarcely a mediæval church which does not display, when the whitewash is removed, traces of work with pious text, sacred picture, or foliated ornament.

In commencing to decorate, the first care of the artist was to cover the surface of the walls with a coating of plaster, sometimes merely forming a thin pellicle to receive the colour. And here we may protest against the destruction, in some of the so-called restorations, of the ancient plastering, exposing thereby the rude rubble walling or filling-in of

[*] See "Glossary of Architecture," vol. iii. p. 7 (Bede, Vita Abb. Wiremuth. et Gew ed Giles. p. 364.

the vaulting; for in no good architecture has a rough surface ever been tolerated for internal work. On this prepared surface the painter worked either in fresco or distemper. Fresco is the term often used to describe these paintings, although it is doubtful whether it was really ever used in England; it is more probable that the colours were applied on the finished plastering, mixed with some glutinous substance, to form a vehicle for the pigments.

In modern works, fresco, distemper, and painting in oil, have been used for wall decorations with varied success; but the science of chemistry is now being applied for the benefit of the painter's art, and fresh vehicles are coming into use, by which he can readily work, and have the command of pigments and refinements in manipulation forbidden to the fresco painter, and by means of which he may hope for a durability scarcely surpassed by the mosaic, which will defy the action of the atmosphere of our manufacturing cities, and the more destructive agency of the cleansing unfortunately necessitated by the soot and dirt which so quickly accumulate on the surface of our walls.

In the designs of the ancient decorations we find that many had their walls simply divided into panels filled with Scriptural and legendary subjects, the arrangement of which was done in a most thoughtful manner, comprising the whole history of the Old and New Testament. To go into the subject would be far beyond the limits of our work. Those who are interested, and wish for further information, will find a most complete account in the admirable "*Manuel d'Iconographie Chrétienne*," published by M. Didron, which contains a complete guide for the painter, taken from a Byzantine manuscript.

A considerable portion of mural decoration, however, consisted of ornamentation, such as diaper work, scrolls with pious texts, representations on the plaster of the jointing of the masonry by lines, painted architectural forms, and tapestry hangings, a brilliant general effect being obtained, not so much by the use of bright colours as by the judicious use of contrast, and sparing use of the most intense pigments, in all cases observing the golden rule of only introducing conventional representations, free from shadow or perspective lines. To disobey this rule is to go beyond the province of the decorator, and to destroy, instead of enhancing, the architecture we desire to adorn. In decoration we must remember that generally the diaper takes the place on the wall of the half-tints of the painter; the background of the architectural features, which we may strengthen, where desirable, by bands of foliage, scrolls, powderings of flowers in gold or bright colours. The lower portion of the walls may be enriched with painted arcades, and the upper part with representations of hangings, thus keeping all strictly in harmony with the architectural lines and detail.

In our illustrations we have not attempted to show much permanent decoration, considering that such decoration must, in every case, be especially designed for the building, under the direction of the architect, and be in accordance with its style and character. The extent to which the decoration is to be carried, the character of the glass in the window, the quantity of light, the description of the furniture, and other circumstances, have also to be taken into consideration in preparing a satisfactory design. These conditions will always be carefully observed by artists who love their work, and who, although living by it, have more than a mere commercial interest in it.

Portions of the work shown, and which may be fitted for permanent decoration, such as scrolls with texts, painted panels, reredoses, &c., are often painted in oil on canvas, or on metal plates. These are very convenient for execution in the studio and workshop by the competent artists that have devoted themselves to the practice of this art.

In general, however, we would suggest a dado of rich colour, serving to protect the walls in the part most generally liable to damage. This, with a cresting of ornament, forms a most appropriate base to the wall-diaper or lining, as before described. The main horizontal lines, such as the strings and wall plates, may have bands with inscriptions, the splays of the windows may have scroll-work; and in all cases, it is a great relief to an interior when the timber of the roof and the spaces between, whether boarded or plastered, are relieved by colour. In roofs of large space, the necessary dimensions of the timber often completely overpower the delicately-moulded arches, and here it is that colour is most valuable, as it enables us to divide and lighten the effect, so as to bring the whole into harmony. A monotonous and heavy roof may be also brightened up easily by having the chamfers painted in a light tint, with small flowers, or by bands of colour and ornament, at irregular distances.

The paintings on metal plates have also the advantage of protection against damp, afforded by the impervious groundwork; and occasionally considerable expense and difficulty, and the use of scaffolding, may be avoided—as, for instance, in panels for ceilings—by the use of prepared canvas, which may easily be fixed to the woodwork or walls, and is, by its preparation, of a durable character. Consideration of distance, and the state of the walls or woodwork, will of course always influence the means employed. All that is here attempted is to call attention to some of the facilities in execution, and the various methods which may be adopted to suit the exigencies of special cases.

Plate 2.

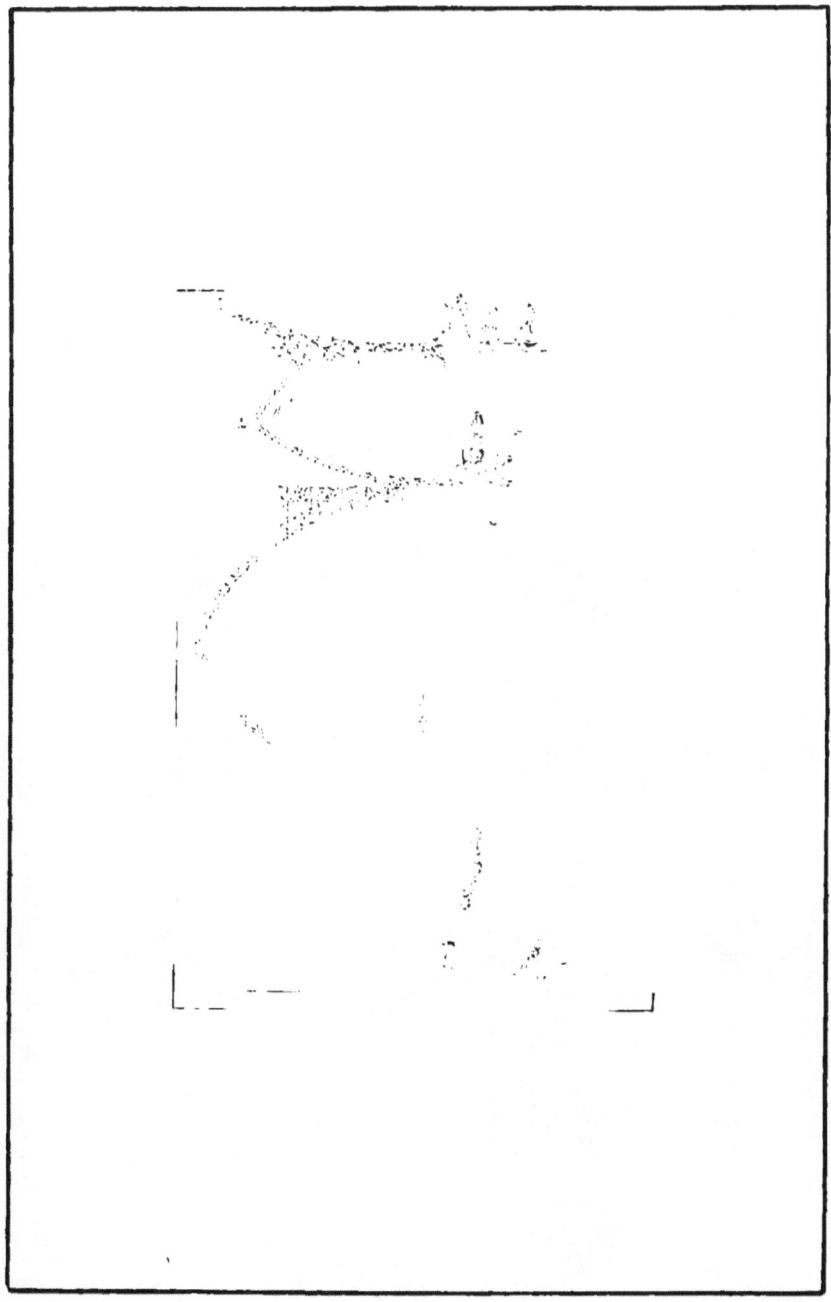

Plate 3.

COX & SONS. LONDON.

Plate 4.

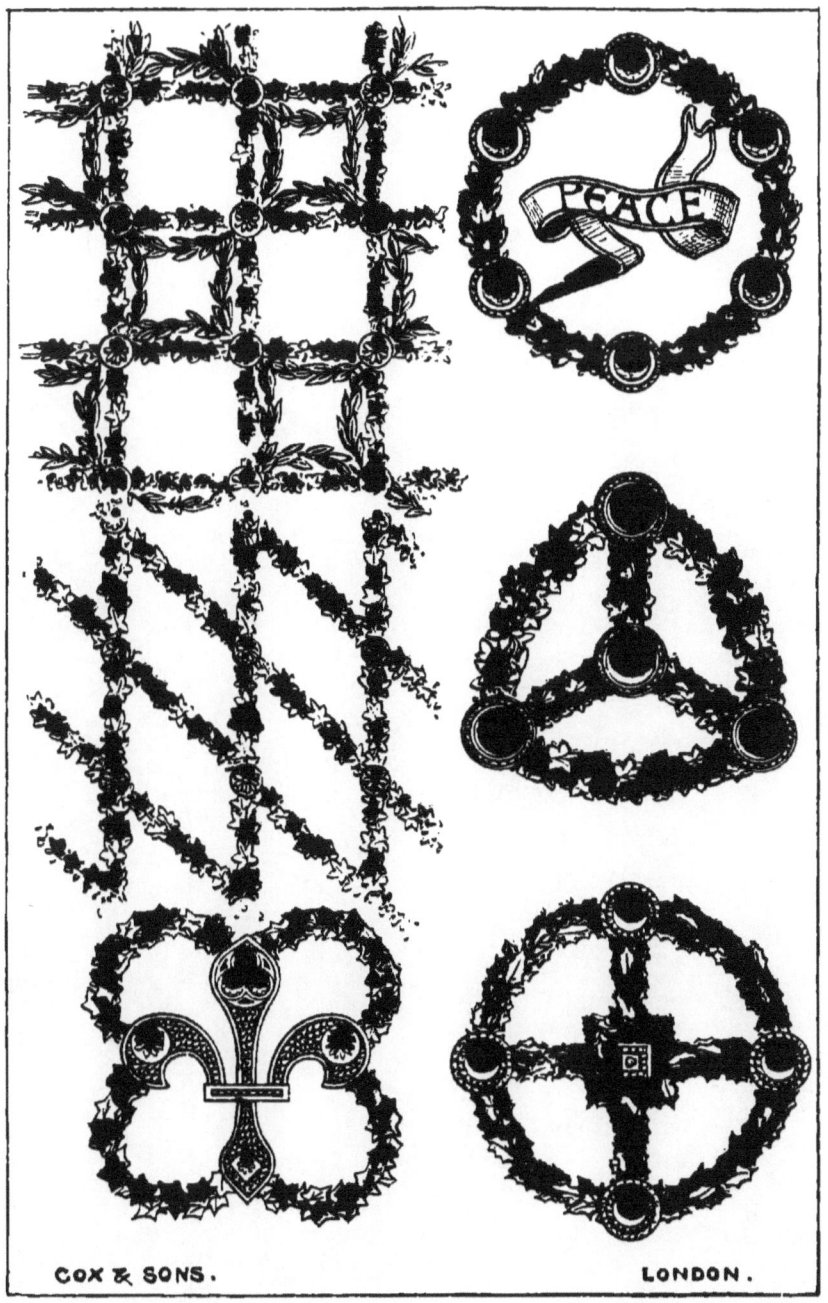

COX & SONS. LONDON.

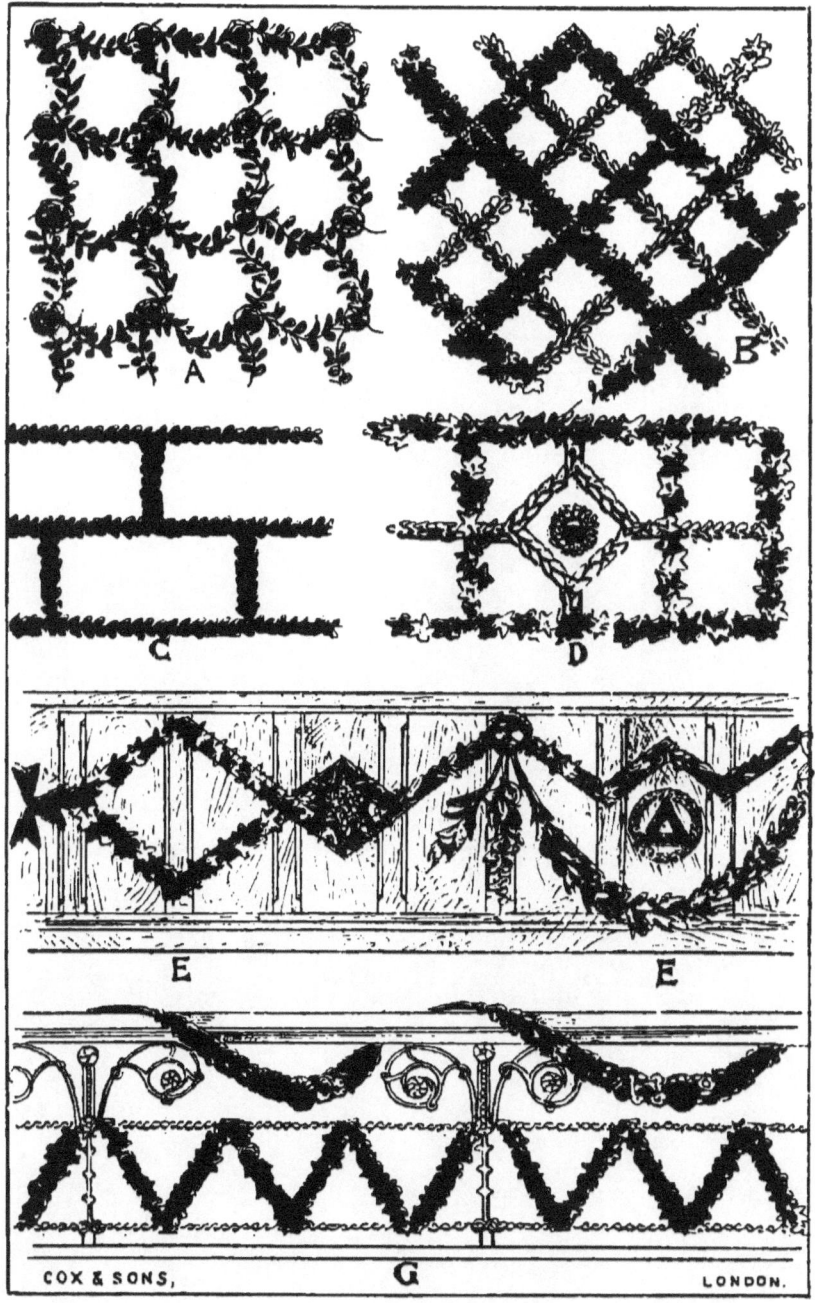

Plate 6

Plate 7.

Plate 8.

Plate 9.

Plate 10

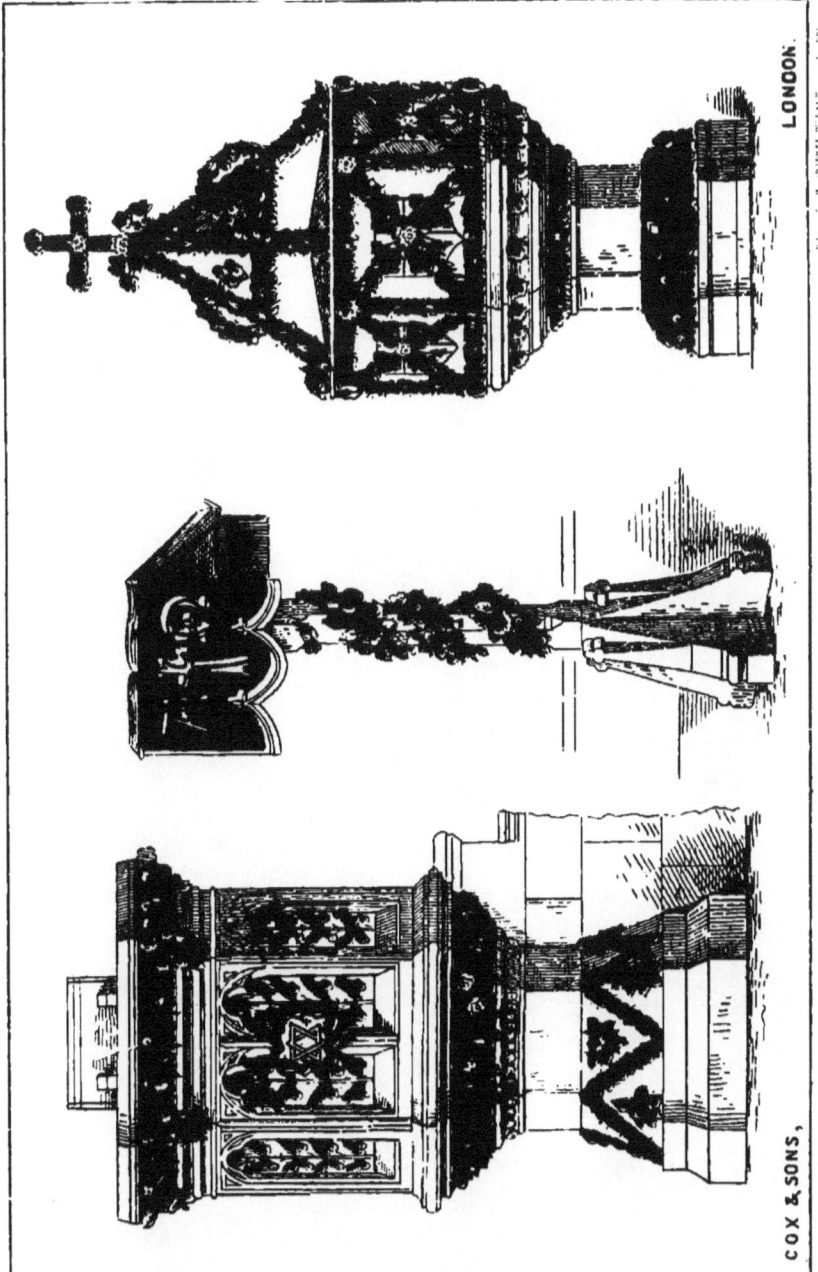

Plate II.

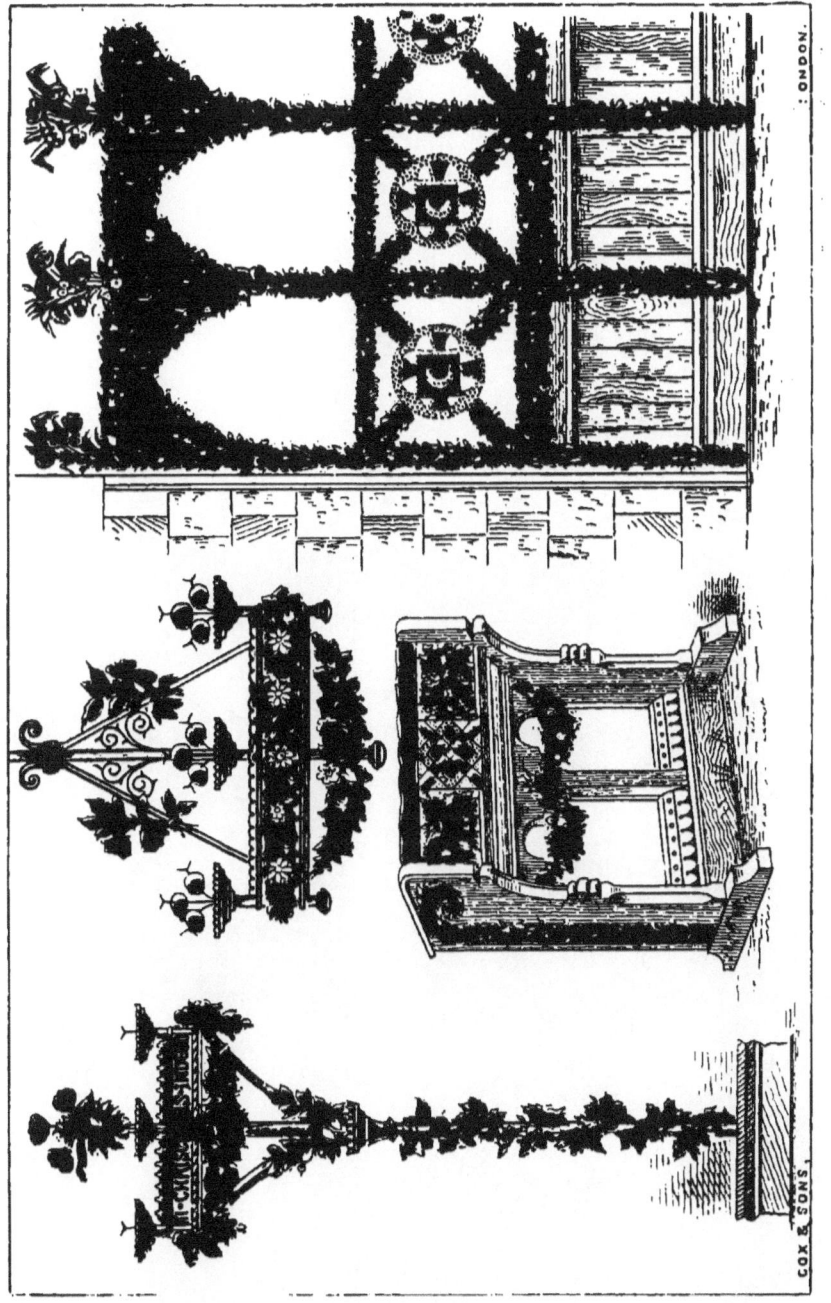

Plate 12.

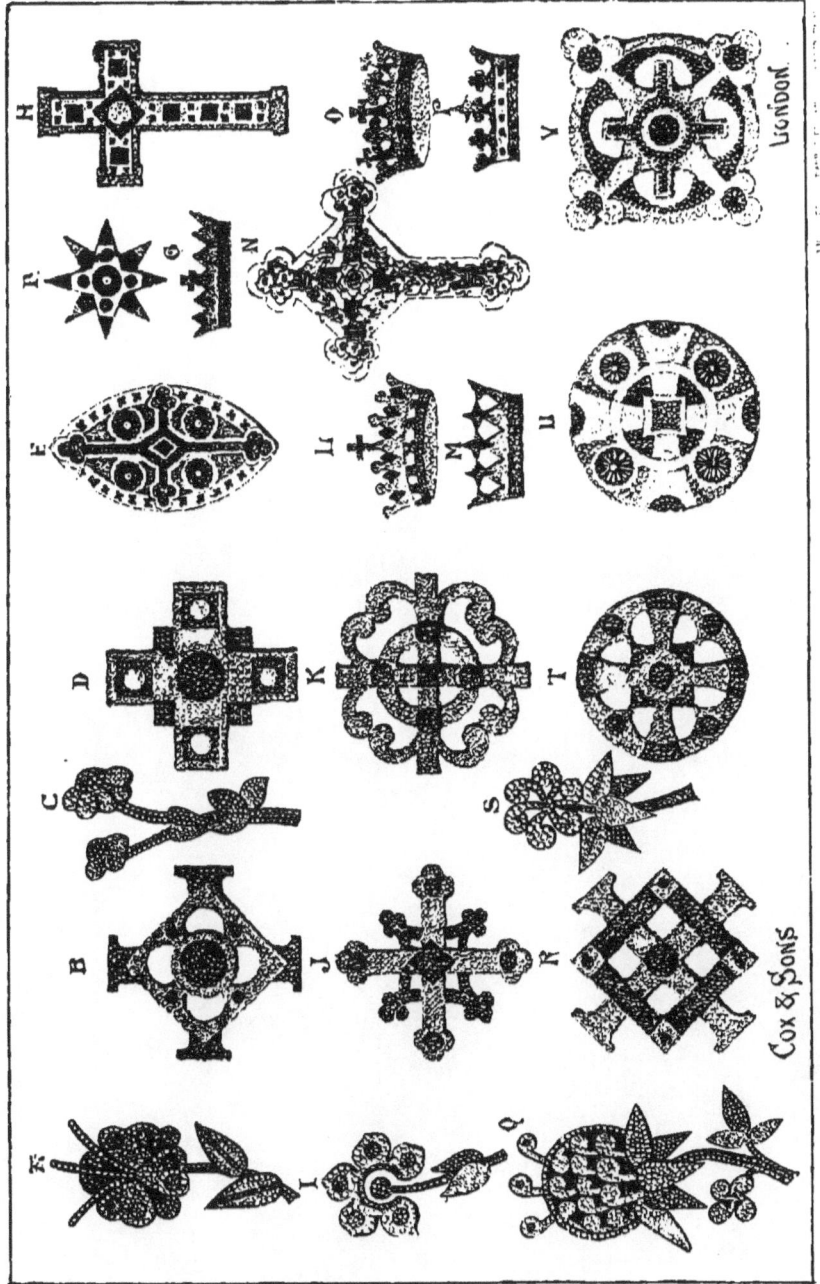

Plate 13

ABCDEFGH
IJKLMNOP
QRSTUVW
XYZ.

abcdefghijkl
mnopqrstuv
wxyz.✝ I·II·III·IV·
V·VI·VII·VIII·IX·X.

COX & SONS   LONDON

ABCDEFG
HIJKLMNO
PQRSTUV
WXYZ.

abcdefghijklmn
opqrstuvwxyz.
1234567890.

Plate 15.

Plate 16

Plate 17.

Plate 18.

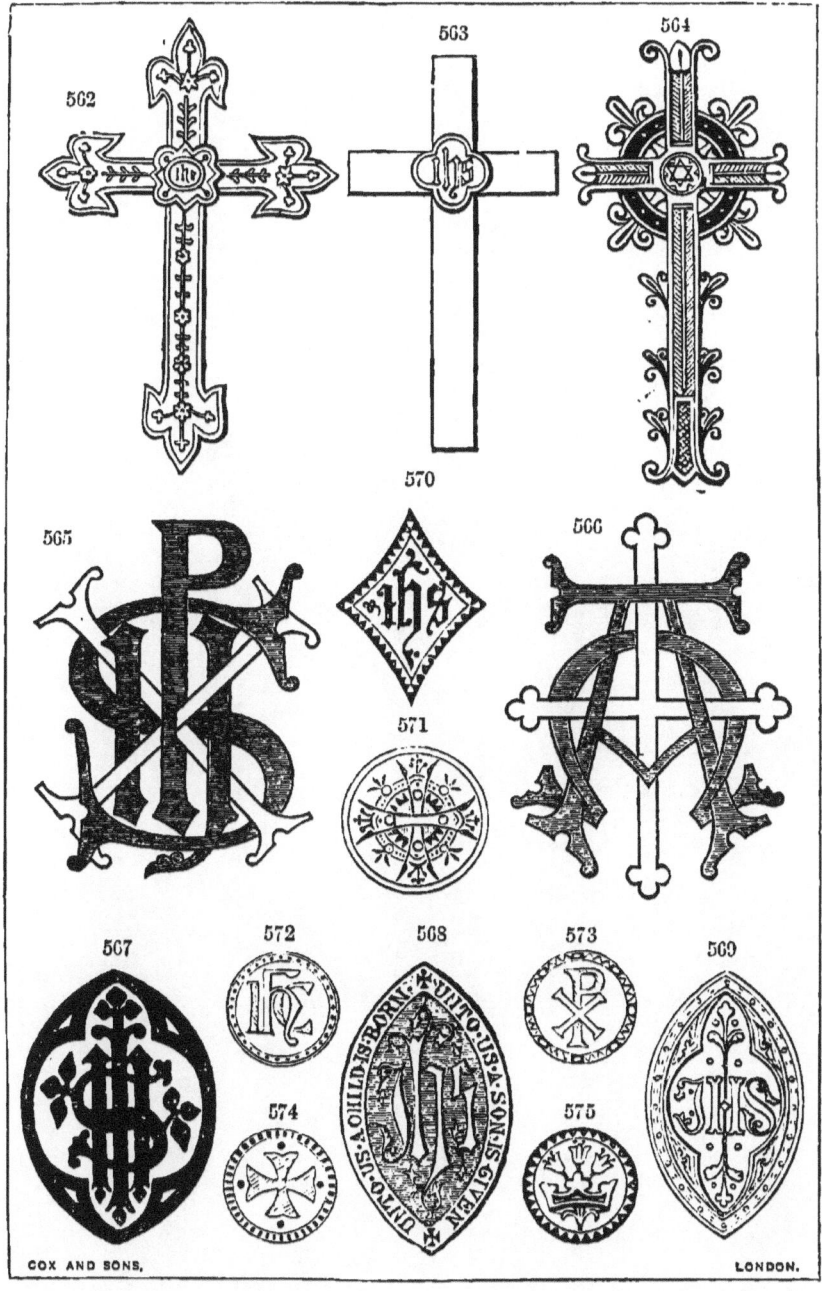

Plate 21.

Plate 22

Plate 23

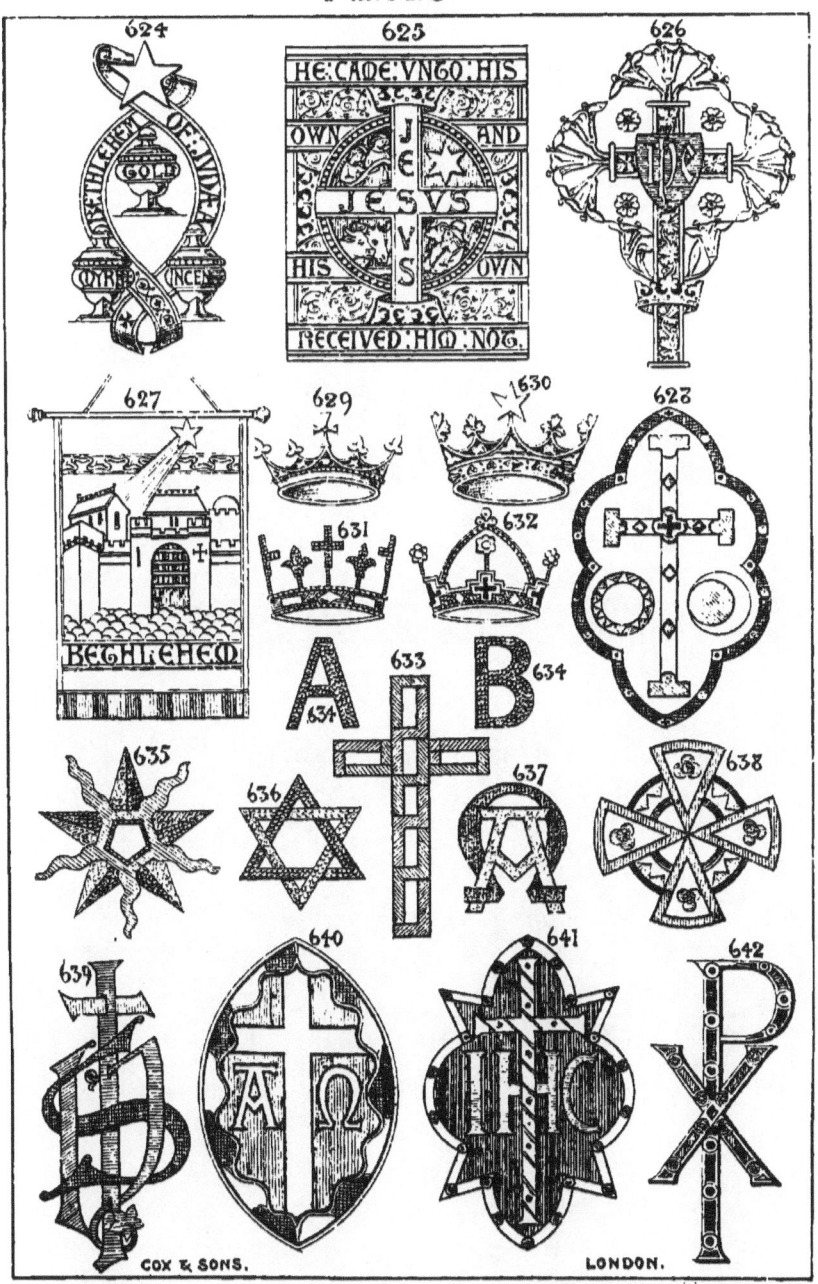

COX & SONS. LONDON.

Plate 24.

Plate 25.

Plate 26

Plate 27

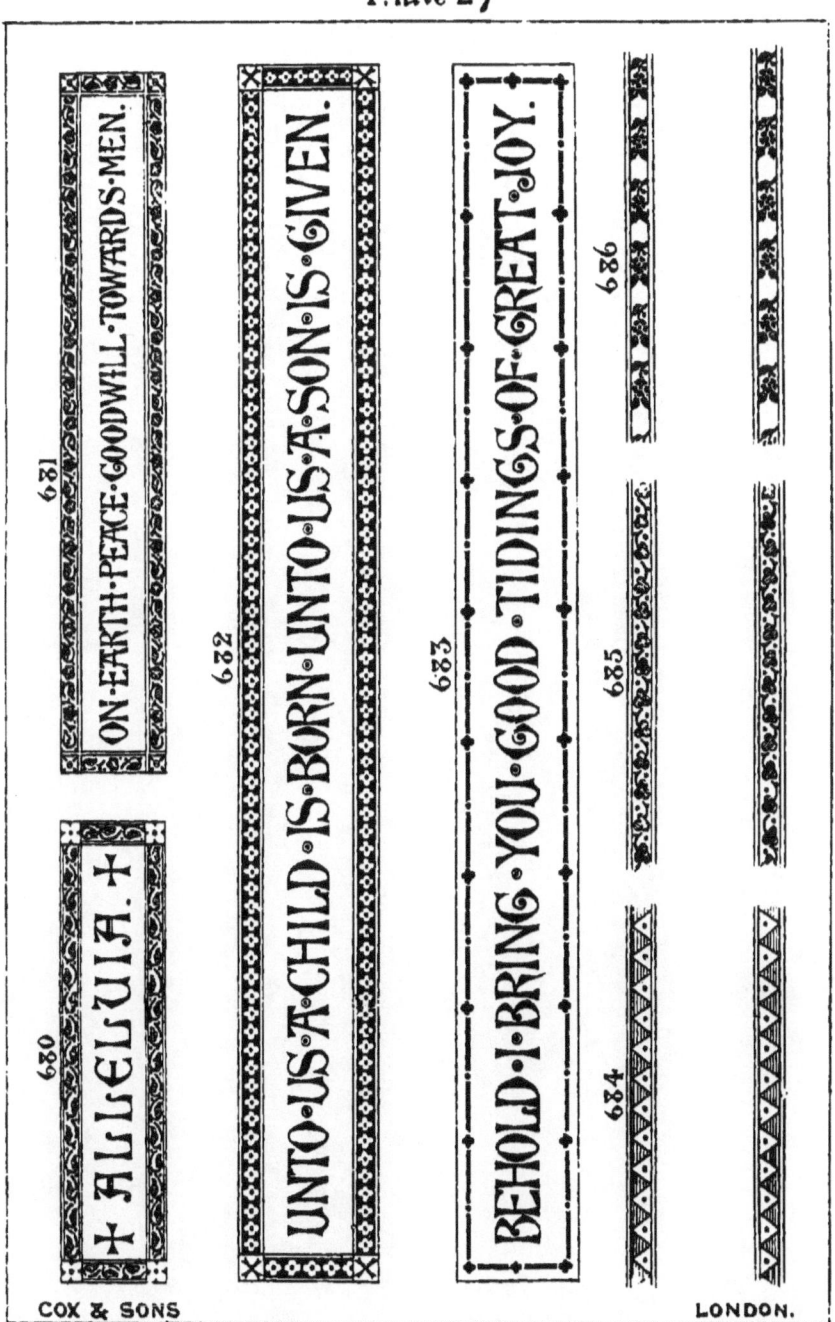

COX & SONS LONDON.

Plate 28

Plate 29.

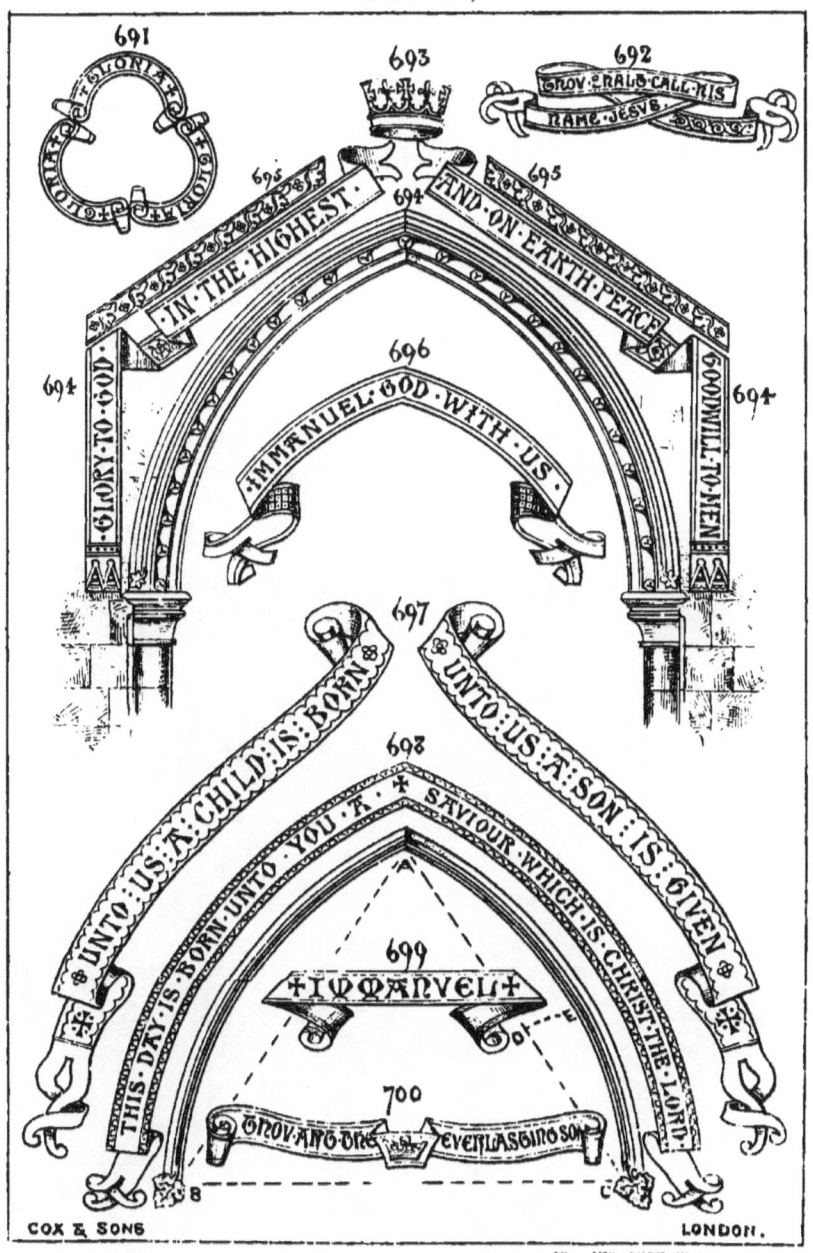

Plate 30.

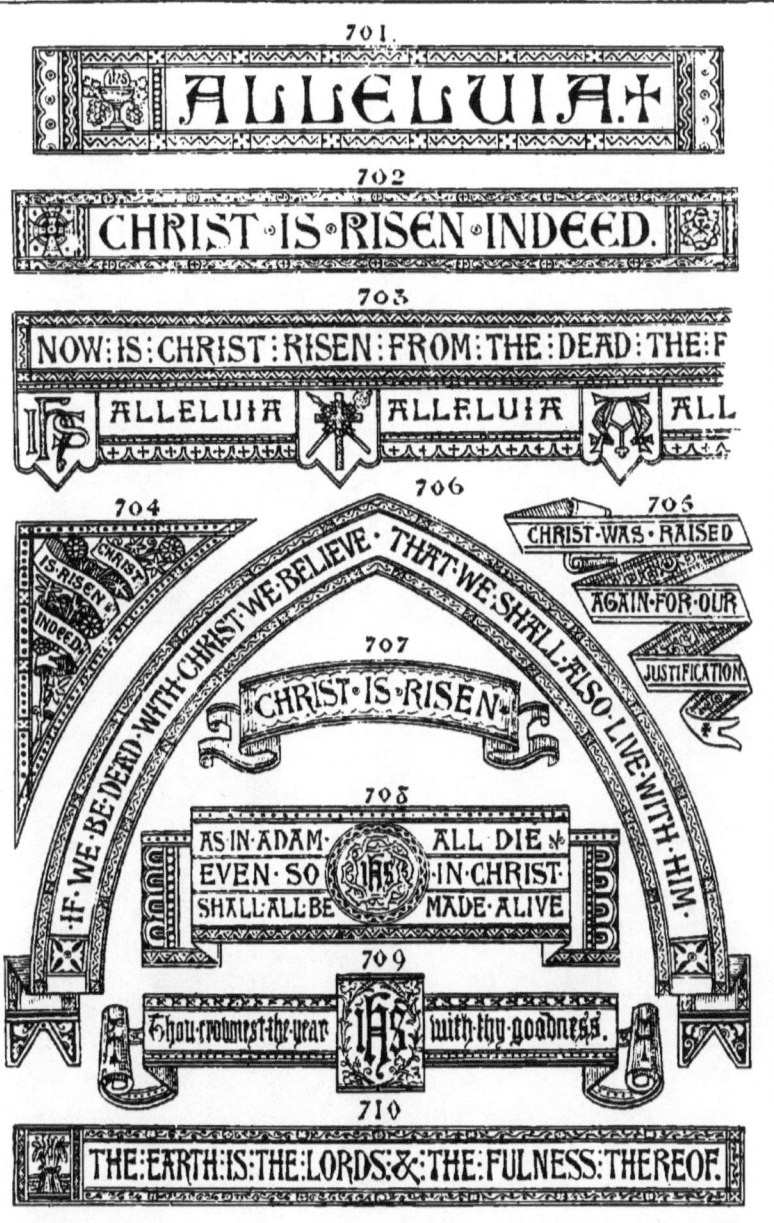

Plate 31.

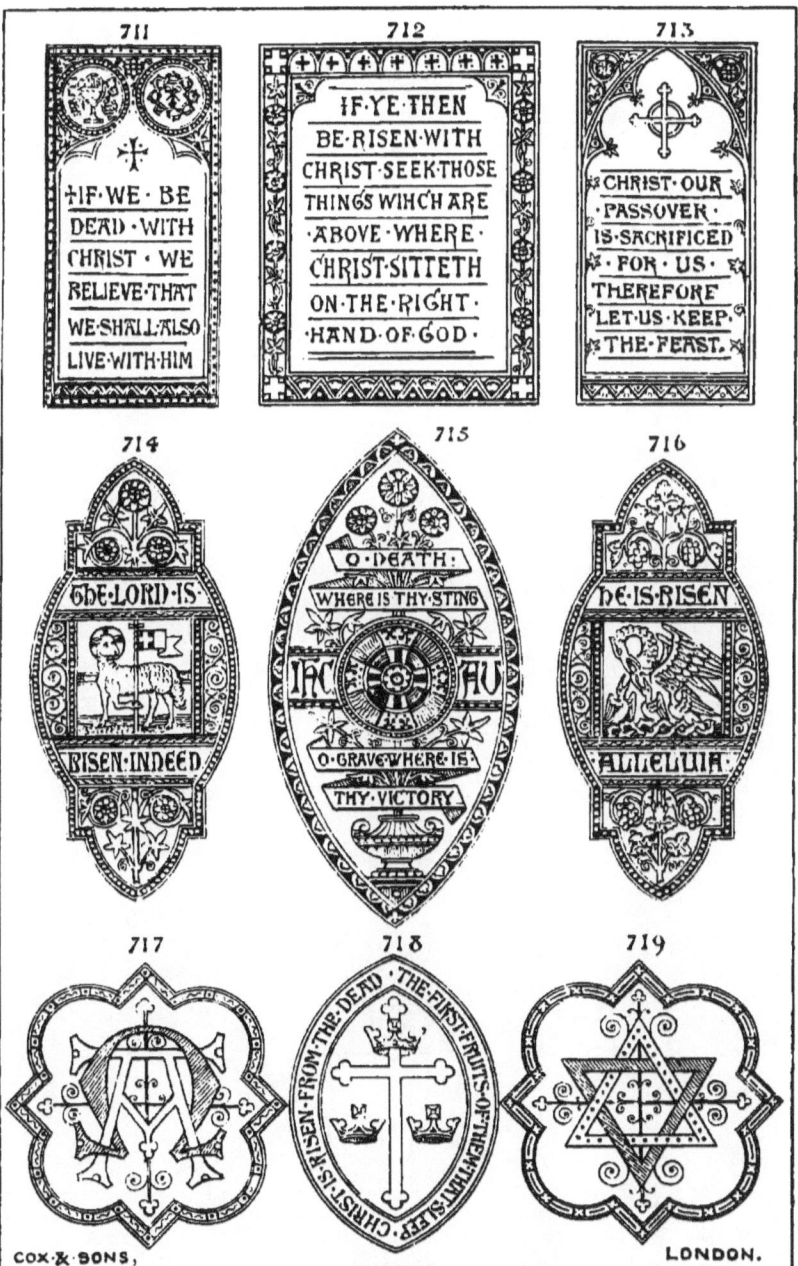

Plate 32

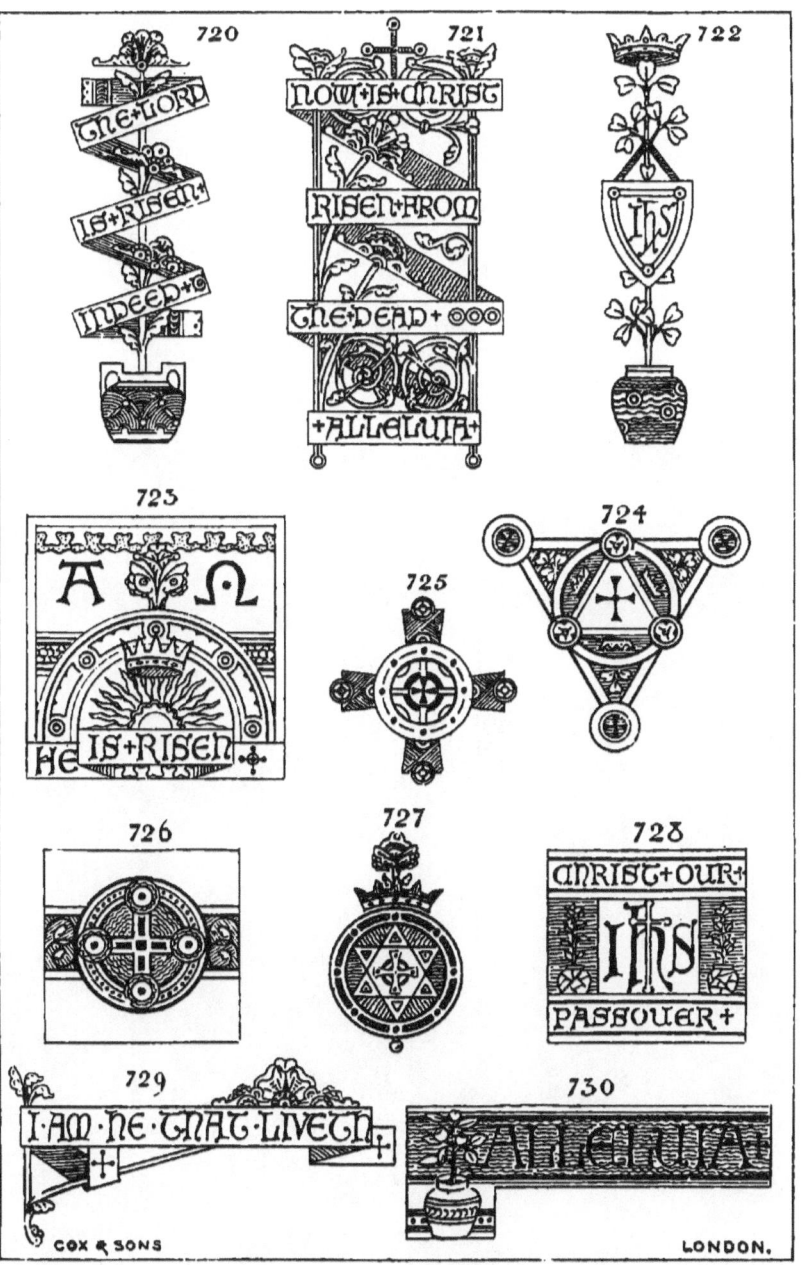

Plate 33.

Plate 34.

734

735

736

Plate 35

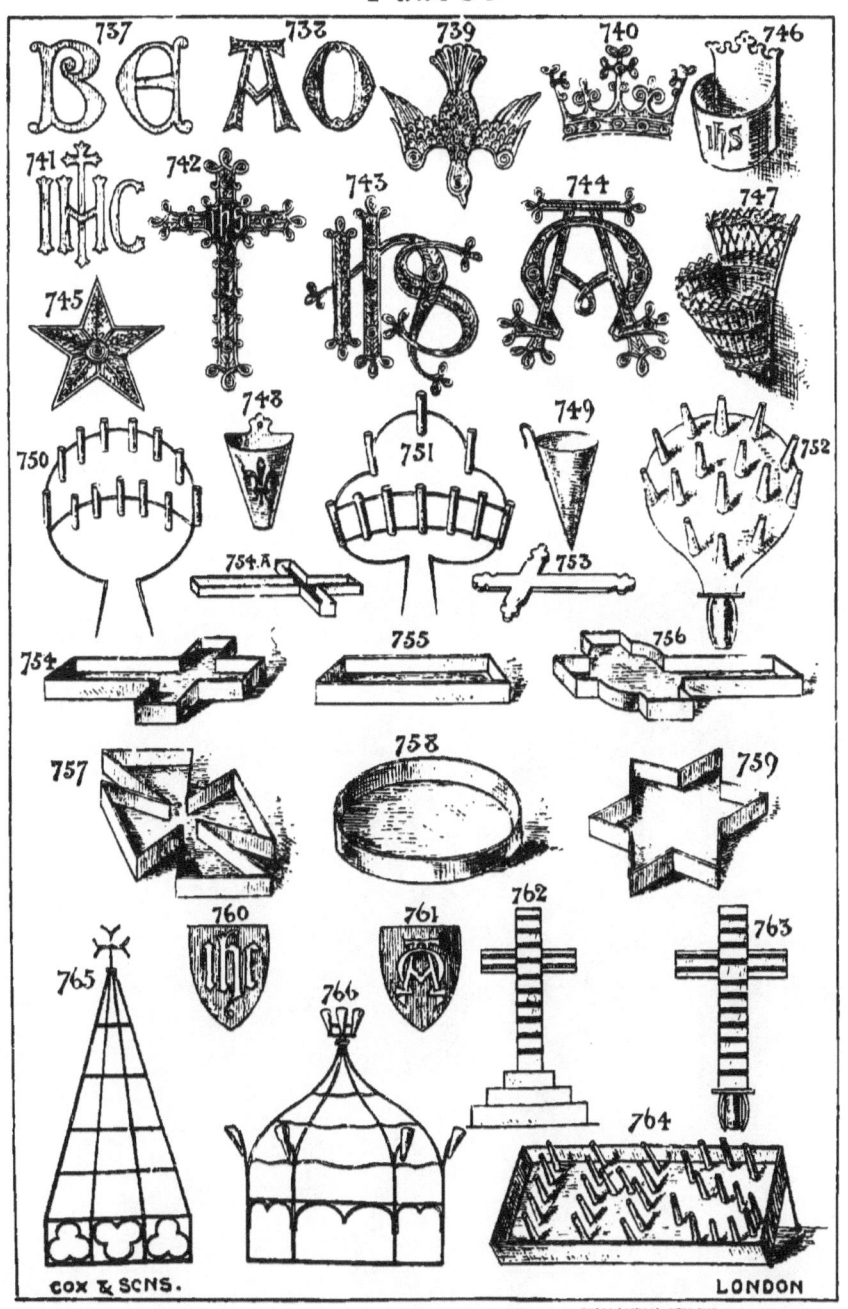

Plate 36.

COX & SONS   LONDON.

Plate 37.

Plate 38.

Plate 39.

Plate 40.

The Author would feel greatly obliged by any Reader kindly making notes on this page, of any suggestions for the improvement of future Editions of this work, and sending them to him; his great aim being to make the Book as thoroughly practical in its instructions as possible.

ADVERTISEMENT.

Messrs COX and SONS beg to submit the following list of prices at which they can supply most of the designs and materials mentioned in the foregoing work.

Owing to the great demand for decorations at Christmas, *it is very desirable that orders should be sent as early as possible,* as more care can be bestowed upon their execution.

In order to afford facilities to those who may desire to do the Illuminated Decorations themselves, the prices are given for the designs sketched in outline only. Those on plates 37, 38, and 39 are specially applicable for this purpose.

N.B.—*The Show-rooms are closed at Two o'clock on Saturdays.*

CARDBOARD LETTERS & PATTERN ALPHABETS.

Letters cut out in Cardboard, as Patterns, or to form Texts.

	Height.	Plain.	Coloured.	Gilt.
No. 500 or 502,	4 inches, per doz.	1/6	2/6	5/
,, ,,	6 ,, ,,	2/	3/	6/6
,, ,,	8 ,, ,,	2/6	4/	7/6
,, ,,	10 ,, ,,	4/	5/6	10/6
,, ,,	12 ,, ,,	5/	7/	14/
501	6 ,, ,,	2/6	3/6	6/6
,,	8 ,, ,,	3/	4/6	8/

Letters under 4 inches charged the same as 4-inch letters. Pattern Alphabets of either of the above charged as two dozen letters, or 3d. extra, post free.

Letters Printed on Paper Assorted.

	Height.	Plain.	Color'd.	Gilt.
No. 500 or 502	4 in., per doz.	/6	1/	3/
500 or 501	6 ,,	1/	1/6	4/
500	8 ,,	1/6	2/6	6/

Printed Alphabets.

	Height.	On Paper.	Cardboard.
No. 500 or 502	4 in.,	1/	1/6
500 or 501	6 ,,	2/	3/
500	8 ,,	3/	4/6

Any Text or Printed Alphabet sent post free for two stamps extra. The above are the only Printed Alphabets and Letters kept in stock; other sizes or patterns would have to be written by hand, and the prices would be the same as for letters cut in Cardboard.

PERFORATED ZINC LETTERS for forming Texts in Berries, Everlasting Flowers, &c.; these being durable, the Texts can be varied from time to time by getting a few extra letters.
No. 503, 4 in. high, 4/; 6 in., 6/; 8 in., 7/6; 10 in., 9/; 12 in., 12/ per dozen.

MONOGRAMS, CROSSES, &c.,

Cut out to shape as a groundwork for Devices in Evergreens, Berries, or Everlasting Flowers.

	IN PERFORATED ZINC.				IN CARDBOARD.			IN LINEN CARTOON PAPER.	
No.	1 ft. high.	1 ft. 6 in. high.	2 ft. high.	2 ft. 6 in. high.	3 ft. high.	1 ft. high.	1 ft. 6 in. high.	2 ft. high.	2 ft. 6 in. high.	3 ft. high.
504	1/	2/	3/	4/	6/	/8	1/	1/6	2/6	3/6
505	2/6	3/6	4/6	5/6	7/6	2/	3/	4/	4/6	6/
506	1/6	2/6	3/6	4/6	6/6	1/	1/6	2/	3/	4/
507	1/6	2/6	3/6	4/6	6/6	1/	1/6	2/	3/	4/
508	1/6	2/6	3/6	4/6	6/6	1/	1/6	2/	3/	4/
509	1/	2/	3/	4/	/8	1/	1/6	2/6	3/6	
510	2/6	3/	4/	5/	7/	1/6	2/6	3/6	4/6	6/
511	1/	2/	3/	4/	6/	/8	1/	1/6	2/6	3/6
512	1/	2/	3/	4/	6/	/8	1/	1/6	2/6	3/6
513	2/6	3/6	4/6	5/6	7/6	2/	3/	4/	4/6	6/
514	2/6	3/6	4/6	5/6	7/6	2/	3/	4/	4/6	6/
515	2/6	3/6	4/6	5/6	7/6	2/	3/	4/	4/6	6/
516	1/	2/	3/	4/	6/	/8	1/	1/6	2/6	3/6
517	2/6	3/6	4/6	5/6	7/6	2/	3/	4/	4/6	6/
518	2/6	3/6	4/6	5/6	7/6	2/	3/	4/	4/6	6/
519	2/6	3/6	4/6	5/6	7/6	2/	3/	4/	4/6	6/
520	1/	2/	3/	4/	6/	/8	1/	1/6	2/6	3/6
521	2/6	3/6	4/6	5/6	7/6	2/	3/	4/	4/6	6/
522	2/6	3/6	4/6	5/6	7/6	2/	3/	4/	4/6	6/
523	1/6	2/6	3/6	4/6	6/6	1/	1/6	2/	3/	4/
524	1/	2/	3/	4/	6/	/8	1/	1/6	2/6	3/6
525	2/	3/	4/	5/	7/	1/6	2/6	3/6	4/6	6/
526	2/	3/	4/	5/	7/	1/6	2/6	3/6	4/6	6/
527	2/	3/	4/	5/	7/	1/6	2/6	3/6	4/6	6/
528	2/6	3/6	4/6	5/6	7/6	2/	3/	4/	4/6	6/
529	3/	4/6	6/	7/6	10/	2/6	3/6	4/6	6/	8/
530	2/6	3/6	4/6	5/6	7/6	2/	3/	4/	4/6	6/
531	2/6	3/6	4/6	5/6	7/6	2/	3/	4/	4/6	6/
532	3/	4/6	6/	7/6	10/	2/6	3/6	4/6	6/	8/
533	2/	3/	4/	5/	7/	1/6	2/6	3/6	4/6	6/
534	2/	3/	4/	5/	7/	1/6	2/6	3/6	4/6	6/
535	2/6	3/6	4/6	5/6	7/6	2/	3/	4/	4/6	6/
536	1/	2/	3/	4/	6/	/8	1/	1/6	2/6	3/6
537*	5/	6/6	8/	10/	13/	3/6	4/6	5/6	7/	9/
538*	5/	6/6	8/	10/	13/	3/6	4/6	5/6	7/	9/
539*	5/	6/6	8/	10/	13/	3/6	4/6	5/6	7/	9/
540*	5/	6/6	8/	10/	13/	3/6	4/6	5/6	7/	9/
541	1/	2/	3/	4/	6/	/8	1/	1/6	2/6	3/6
542	1/	2/	3/	4/	6/	/8	1/	1/6	2/6	3/6
543	1/6	2/6	3/6	4/6	6/6	1/	1/6	2/	3/	4/
544	2/	3/	4/	5/	7/	1/6	2/6	3/6	4/6	6/
545	1/	2/	3/	4/	6/	/8	1/	1/6	2/6	3/6

* The centres of Nos. 537, 538, 539, and 540 are illuminated in colours.

No.	PERFORATED ZINC CROWNS. Extreme Length.					CARDBOARD CROWNS. Extreme Length.				
	8 in.	1 ft.	1 ft. 6 in.	2 ft.	2 ft. 6 in.	8 in.	1 ft.	1 ft. 6 in.	2 ft.	2 ft. 6 in.
546	1/	1/6	2/6	3/6	4/6	/8	1/	1/6	2/	3/
547	1/6	2/	3/	4/	5/	1/	1/6	2/3	3/	4/
548	1/6	2/	3/	4/	5/	1/	1/6	2/3	3/	4/
549	1/6	2/	3/	4/	5/	1/	1/6	2/3	3/	4/

The above prices are for flat crowns; if made circular, they would be three times as much as quoted.

Any of the Devices on Plates 15 and 16 can be supplied painted a deep crimson colour on cardboard, as centres for evergreen and other devices, at the same prices as are quoted for them in Perforated Zinc.

ILLUMINATED MONOGRAMS, CROSSES, AND DEVICES.

No.	1 ft. high.				1 ft. 6 in. high.				2 ft. high.			
	ON CARDBOARD OR PREPARED CALICO.		ON PREPARED CLOTH.		ON CARDBOARD OR PREPARED CALICO.		ON PREPARED CLOTH.		ON CARDBOARD OR PREPARED CALICO.		ON PREPARED CLOTH.	
	Plainly Illuminated in Colours.	Richly Illuminated in Colours & Gold.	Outlined ready for Illumination.	Plainly Illuminated in Colours.	Richly Illuminated in Colours & Gold.	Outlined ready for Illumination.	Plainly Illuminated in Colours.	Richly Illuminated in Colours & Gold.	Outlined ready for Illumination.	Plainly Illuminated in Colours.	Richly Illuminated in Colours & Gold.	Outlined ready for Illumination.
550	2/9	3/9	1/6	4/6	6/	3/	3/6	4/6	2/	5/6	7/	3/6	4/6	6/	3/	7/	9/	4/6
551	4/	5/6	2/6	6/	8/	3/6	5/	6/6	3/	7/	9/	4/6	6/	7/6	3/6	8/6	10/6	5/
552	2/9	3/9	1/6	4/6	6/	3/	3/6	5/	2/	5/6	7/6	3/6	4/6	6/	3/	7/	9/	4/6
553	3/6	5/	2/	5/6	7/6	3/6	4/6	6/	2/6	6/6	8/6	4/	5/6	7/	3/6	8/	10/	5/
554	6/6	8/6	3/6	9/	11/6	5/	8/	10/	4/	10/6	13/	6/	10/	12/6	5/	12/6	16/	7/6
555	4/6	6/	3/	6/6	8/6	4/6	5/6	7/6	3/6	8/	10/6	5/	7/6	9/6	4/	10/6	13/	6/6
556	3/6	5/	2/	5/6	7/6	3/6	4/6	6/	2/6	6/6	8/6	4/	5/6	7/	3/6	8/	10/	5/
557	4/6	6/	3/	6/6	8/6	4/6	5/6	7/6	3/6	8/	10/6	5/	7/6	9/6	4/	10/6	13/	6/6
558	5/	7/	3/	7/6	10/	4/6	6/6	8/6	3/6	9/	11/6	5/6	8/6	10/6	4/6	11/6	14/	7/
559	5/	7/	3/	7/6	10/	4/6	6/6	8/6	3/6	9/	11/6	5/6	8/6	10/6	4/6	11/6	14/	7/
560	5/6	7/6	3/6	8/	11/	5/	7/	9/	4/	9/6	12/	6/	9/	11/	5/	12/	14/6	7/6
561	6/	8/	3/6	8/6	11/6	5/	7/6	10/	4/	10/6	13/	6/	9/6	11/6	5/	13/	15/6	7/6
562	5/6	7/6	3/6	8/	11/	4/6	7/	9/	4/	9/6	12/	6/	9/	11/	5/	12/	14/6	7/
563	2/	3/	1/	3/6	5/6	2/	2/6	3/6	1/6	4/	6/	2/6	3/6	4/6	2/	5/	7/	3/6
564	6/6	8/6	4/	9/	12/	5/6	8/	10/	4/6	10/6	13/6	6/6	10/	12/	5/6	12/6	15/6	7/6
565	3/6	5/	2/	5/6	7/6	3/6	4/6	6/	2/6	6/6	8/6	4/6	5/6	7/	3/6	8/	10/	5/
566	3/6	5/	2/	5/6	7/6	3/6	4/6	6/	2/6	6/6	8/6	4/6	5/6	7/	3/6	8/	10/	5/
567	4/6	6/	3/	6/6	8/6	4/6	5/6	7/6	3/6	8/	11/	5/6	7/6	9/6	4/	10/6	13/	6/6
568	7/6	9/6	5/	10/6	13/6	6/6	9/	11/	5/6	12/6	15/6	8/	11/6	13/6	6/6	15/6	18/6	9/6

569. Woven Silk Monogram 15 inches high, 7/6
570.   ,,   ,,   ,,   10   ,,   2/6
571.   ,,   ,,   Cross   4   ,,   2/6

Monograms and Devices Illuminated on Silk for Appliqué Work.

572. 6 inches diameter 5/   9 inches diameter 6/
573. 6   ,,   ,, 5/   9 ,,   ,, 6/
574. 6   ,,   ,, 4/6   9 ,,   ,, 5/6
575. 6   ,,   ,, 5/6   9 ,,   ,, 6/6

ILLUMINATED MONOGRAMS, CROSSES, AND DEVICES.

No.	1 ft. high. ON CALICO. Plainly Illuminated in Colours.	1 ft. high. ON CALICO. Richly Illuminated in Colours & Gold.	1 ft. high. ON CALICO. Outlined ready for Illumination.	1 ft. high. ON PREPARED CLOTH. Plainly Illuminated in Colours.	1 ft. high. ON PREPARED CLOTH. Richly Illuminated in Colours & Gold.	1 ft. high. ON PREPARED CLOTH. Outlined ready for Illumination.	1 ft. 6 in. high. ON CALICO. Plainly Illuminated in Colours.	1 ft. 6 in. high. ON CALICO. Richly Illuminated in Colours & Gold.	1 ft. 6 in. high. ON CALICO. Outlined ready for Illumination.	1 ft. 6 in. high. ON PREPARED CLOTH. Plainly Illuminated in Colours.	1 ft. 6 in. high. ON PREPARED CLOTH. Richly Illuminated in Colours & Gold.	1 ft. 6 in. high. ON PREPARED CLOTH. Outlined ready for Illumination.	2 ft. high. ON CALICO. Plainly Illuminated in Colours.	2 ft. high. ON CALICO. Richly Illuminated in Colours & Gold.	2 ft. high. ON CALICO. Outlined ready for Illumination.	2 ft. high. ON PREPARED CLOTH. Plainly Illuminated in Colours.	2 ft. high. ON PREPARED CLOTH. Richly Illuminated in Colours & Gold.	2 ft. high. ON PREPARED CLOTH. Outlined ready for Illumination.
600	2/6	3/6	1/6	4/	5/6	2/	3/	4/6	2/	5/	6/6	3/	4/	5/6	2/6	6/	8/	4/
601	5/6	7/6	3/6	8/	10/6	5/	7/6	9/6	4/	10/	12/6	6/	9/6	11/6	5/6	12/6	15/6	8/
602	3/6	5/	2/	5/6	7/6	3/	4/6	6/	2/6	6/6	8/6	4/	5/6	7/	3/6	8/	10/	5/
603	6/6	8/6	3/6	9/	12/	5/	8/	10/6	4/6	11/6	14/6	6/6	10/6	13/	5/6	14/	17/6	8/
604	6/	8/	3/6	8/6	11/6	5/	7/6	10/	4/	10/6	13/6	6/	9/6	11/6	5/	13/	16/	7/6
605	6/	8/	3/6	8/6	11/6	5/	7/6	10/	4/	10/6	13/6	6/	9/6	11/6	5/	13/	16/	7/6
606	6/6	8/6	4/	9/	11/6	5/6	8/	10/6	4/6	10/6	13/6	6/6	10/	12/	5/6	13/6	16/6	8/
607	8/6	10/6	4/6	11/6	14/6	6/6	10/	12/	5/6	13/6	16/6	7/6	12/6	15/6	7/	17/	20/	9/
608	6/6	8/6	4/	9/	11/6	5/6	8/	10/6	4/6	10/6	13/6	6/6	10/	12/6	5/6	13/6	16/6	8/
609	6/6	8/6	4/	9/	11/6	5/6	8/	10/6	4/6	10/6	13/6	6/6	10/	12/6	5/6	13/6	16/6	8/

No.	2 ft. diameter. ON CALICO. Plainly	2 ft. diameter. ON CALICO. Richly	2 ft. diameter. ON CALICO. Outlined	2 ft. diameter. ON PREPARED CLOTH. Plainly	2 ft. diameter. ON PREPARED CLOTH. Richly	2 ft. diameter. ON PREPARED CLOTH. Outlined	2 ft. 6 in. diameter. ON CALICO. Plainly	2 ft. 6 in. diameter. ON CALICO. Richly	2 ft. 6 in. diameter. ON CALICO. Outlined	2 ft. 6 in. diameter. ON PREPARED CLOTH. Plainly	2 ft. 6 in. diameter. ON PREPARED CLOTH. Richly	2 ft. 6 in. diameter. ON PREPARED CLOTH. Outlined	3 ft. diameter. ON CALICO. Plainly	3 ft. diameter. ON CALICO. Richly	3 ft. diameter. ON CALICO. Outlined	3 ft. diameter. ON PREPARED CLOTH. Plainly	3 ft. diameter. ON PREPARED CLOTH. Richly	3 ft. diameter. ON PREPARED CLOTH. Outlined
610	10/	12/6	6/6	14/6	18/	9/	13/6	16/6	7/6	18/6	22/6	10/6	17/6	21/	9/	23/6	28/	13/6
611	10/	12/6	6/6	14/6	18/	9/	13/6	16/6	7/6	18/6	22/6	10/6	17/6	21/	9/	23/6	28/	13/6

No.	Height. ft. in.	ON CALICO. Plainly Illuminated in Colours.	ON CALICO. Richly Illuminated in Colours and Gold.	ON CALICO. Outlined ready for Illumination.	ON PREPARED CLOTH. Plainly Illuminated in Colours.	ON PREPARED CLOTH. Richly Illuminated in Colours and Gold.	ON PREPARED CLOTH. Outlined ready for Illumination.	Height. ft. in.	ON CALICO. Plainly Illuminated in Colours.	ON CALICO. Richly Illuminated in Colours and Gold.	ON CALICO. Outlined ready for Illumination.	ON PREPARED CLOTH. Plainly Illuminated in Colours.	ON PREPARED CLOTH. Richly Illuminated in Colours and Gold.	ON PREPARED CLOTH. Outlined ready for Illumination.
612	3 0	16/	20/	9/	21/	26/	13/6	5 0	21/	25/	12/	30/	35/	17/6
613	3 0	16/	20/	9/	21/	26/	13/6	5 0	21/	25/	12/	30/	35/	17/6
614	3 0	16/	20/	9/	21/	26/	13/6	5 0	21/	25/	12/	30/	35/	17/6
615	3 0	16/	20/	9/	21/	26/	13/6	5 0	21/	25/	12/	30/	35/	17/6
616	3 0	14/6	18/6	8/	20/	25/	11/6	5 0	19/	23/	11/6	26/	31/6	17/
617	1 6	9/	11/	5/6	12/	15/	7/6	2 6	14/6	17/	7/6	18/	21/	11/
618	1 6	9/	11/	5/6	12/	15/	7/6	2 6	14/6	17/	7/6	18/	21/	11/
619	1 6	8/	10/	5/	11/6	14/6	7/	2 6	11/6	14/	6/6	16/	20/	10/
620	1 6	8/	10/	5/	11/6	14/6	7/	2 6	11/6	14/	6/6	16/	20/	10/
	length. ft. in.							length. ft. in						
621	3 0	8/6	10/6	6/	12/6	15/6	8/	5 0	12/6	15/6	8/6	17/6	21/	11/6
622	3 0	9/6	12/	6/6	13/6	17/	9/	5 0	14/	17/6	9/	19/	24/	13/

623 Texts for encircling Columns in long lengths on Prepared Calico, 2/ per yard; on Prepared Cloth, 3/ per yard.

ILLUMINATED DEVICES.

No. and Height		ON CALICO.			ON PREPARED CLOTH.		
		Plainly Illuminated in Colours.	Richly Illuminated in Colours & Gold.	Outlined ready for Illumination	Plainly Illuminated in Colours.	Richly Illuminated in Colours & Gold.	Outlined ready for Illumination
624.	2 ft.	11/	15/	7/	15/	19/6	9/6
,,	3 ft.	15/	19/	8/6	19/	24/	11/6
625.	2 ft.	17/	22/	10/	21/	26/	14/
,,	3 ft.	21/	27/	12/	26/	33/	16/6
626.	2 ft.	12/	16/	8/	16/	21/	9/6
,,	3 ft.	16/	20/	9/6	20/	26/	12/6
627.	2 ft.	14/	17/	8/6	18/	22/	12/6
,,	3 ft.	17/	21/	9/6	21/	25/	14/

ILLUMINATED CARDBOARD CROWNS.

	Illuminated	Extreme Length.			
		8 in.	1 ft.	1 ft. 6.	2 ft.
629.	Plainly,	2/	2/6	3/6	4/6
,,	Richly,	3/	3/6	5/	6/
630.	Plainly,	2/6	3/	4/	5/
,,	Richly,	3/6	4/	5/6	6/6

DEVICES FORMED IN EVERLASTINGS, in Two or more Colours.

628.	18 in. high,	15/	...	24 in. high,	25/
631.	9 in. long,	4/6	...	12 in. long,	6/
632.	,, ,,	4/	...	,, ,,	5/6
633.	12 ,,	3/	...	15 ,,	3/6
634.	18 ,,	4/6	...	24 ,,	6/

LETTERS FORMED IN EVERLASTING FLOWERS, in two Colours.

	6 in. high, 18/ per doz.			8 in. high, 24/ per doz.	
635.	8 in.,	3/6	...	12 in.,	7/
636.	8 ,,	3/6	...	12 ,,	7/
637.	8 ,,	3/6	...	12 ,,	7/
638.	8 ,,	3/6	...	12 ,,	7/
639.	12 ,,	7/6	...	18 ,,	10/6
640.	12 ,,	9/	...	18 ,,	13/6
641.	12 ,,	10/	...	18 ,,	15/
642.	12 ,,	6/6	...	18 ,,	9/

ILLUMINATED BANNERS.

	ON PREPARED CALICO.						ON PREPARED CLOTH.		
	2 ft. 2 by 1 ft. 4.			3 ft. by 1 ft. 10.			2 ft. 2 by 1 ft. 4.			3 ft. by 1 ft. 10.		
No.	Plainly Illuminated in Colours.	Richly Illuminated in Colours and Gold.	Outlined ready for Illumination.	Plainly Illuminated in Colours.	Richly Illuminated in Colours and Gold.	Outlined ready for Illumination.	Plainly Illuminated in Colours.	Richly Illuminated in Colours and Gold.	Outlined ready for Illumination.	Plainly Illuminated in Colours.	Richly Illuminated in Colours and Gold.	Outlined ready for Illumination.
643	6/6	8/	4/6	9/	11/	6/6	9/	11/	5/6	12/6	15/	7/6
*644	5/	6/6	4/	7/	9/	5/6	7/	9/	5/	10/6	13/	6/6
*645	6/	7/6	4/6	8/	10/	6/	8/	10/	5/6	11/6	14/	7/
646	7/	9/	5/	10/	12/	7/	10/	12/	6/	14/	16/6	8/6
647	7/	9/	5/	10/	12/	7/	10/	12/	6/	14/	16/6	8/6
648	6/6	8/	4/6	9/	11/	6/6	9/	11/	5/6	12/6	15/	7/6
649	11/6	13/6	7/6	14/6	17/	9/6	15/	17/6	9/	19/	22/	11/6
650	17/6	21/	11/6	21/	25/	13/6	22/	26/	13/6	26/	31/6	16/
651	17/6	21/	11/6	21/	25/	13/6	22/	26/	13/6	26/	31/6	16/
652	17/6	21/	11/6	21/	25/	13/6	22/	26/	13/6	26/	31/6	16/
653	16/6	20/	10/6	20/	24/	12/6	21/	25/	12/6	25/	30/	15/
654	11/6	13/6	7/6	14/6	17/	9/6	15/	17/6	9/	19/	22/	11/6
655	16/6	20/	10/6	20/	24/	12/6	21/	25/	12/6	25/	30/	15/

* The pointed-shaped banners Nos. 644 and 645 are longer than the sizes quoted above.

ILLUMINATED BANNERS.

No.	ON PREPARED CALICO.						ON PREPARED CLOTH.					
	2 ft. by 1 ft. 4.			3 ft. by 1 ft. 10.			2 ft. 2 by 1 ft. 4.			3 ft. by 1 ft. 10.		
	Plainly Illuminated in Colours.	Richly Illuminated in Colours and Gold.	Outlined ready for Illumination.	Plainly Illuminated in Colours.	Richly Illuminated in Colours and Gold.	Outlined ready for Illumination.	Plainly Illuminated in Colours.	Richly Illuminated in Colours and Gold.	Outlined ready for Illumination.	Plainly Illuminated in Colours.	Richly Illuminated in Colours and Gold.	Outlined ready for Illumination.
656	3/6	6/	2/6	5/	8/	3/6	5/	8/	3/6	7/	10/6	5/
657	3/6	6/	2/6	5/	8/	3/6	5/	8/	3/6	7/	10/6	5/
658	3/6	6/	2/6	5/	8/	3/6	5/	8/	3/6	7/	10/6	5/
659	7/	9/	5/	10/	12/	7/	10/	12/	6/	14/	16/6	8/6
660	6/6	8/	4/6	9/	11/	6/6	9/	11/	5/6	12/6	15/	7/6
661	6/6	8/	4/6	9/	11/	6/6	9/	11/	5/6	12/6	15/	7/6
662	10/6	12/6	6/6	13/6	16/	8/6	14/	16/6	8/	18/	21/	10/6
663	10/6	12/6	6/6	13/6	16/	8/6	14/	16/6	8/	18/	21/	10/6
664	11/6	13/6	7/6	14/6	17/	9/6	15/	17/6	9/	19/	22/	11/6
665	10/6	12/6	6/6	13/6	16/	8/6	14/	16/6	8/	18/	21/	10/6
666	10/6	12/6	6/6	13/6	16/	8/6	14/	16/6	8/	18/	21/	10/6
667	7/6	9/6	5/	10/6	12/6	7/	10/6	12/6	6/	14/6	17/	8/6
668	15/	17/6	9/	18/	21/	11/	19/	22/	10/6	23/	27/	11/6
669	11/	13/	7/6	14/	16/6	9/	14/6	17/6	9/	18/6	22/	11/6
670	15/	17/6	9/	18/	21/	11/	19/	22/	10/6	23/	27/	11/6
671	10/6	12/6	6/6	13/6	16/	8/6	14/	16/6	8/	18/	21/	10/6
672	18/	23/	10/6	22/	27/	14/	21/	26/	12/	24/	30/	15/6
673	15/	17/6	9/	18/	21/	11/	19/	22/	10/6	23/	27/	11/6

674. White or Coloured Rep Banner, 3 ft. by 2 feet, with Woven Silk Monogram, Silk Fringe and Cord, 21s.
675. Rep Banner, 3 ft. by 2 feet, with Silk Appliqué and Fringe, 25s.
676. Appliqué Silk Banner, 3 ft. by 2 ft., 50s.

BANNERS IN STRAW-WORK.
MOUNTED ON COTTON VELVET.

677.	30 in. by 20 in.,	.	27/	36 in. by 24 in.,	.	35/
678.	,,	,,	.	21/	,,	,,	.	30/
679.	,,	,,	.	21/	,,	,,	.	30/

The quotations for banners do not include poles or cord. Cross poles painted blue with gilt ends, including cord, are 3/6; or with coloured ends, 2/6 each. Upright poles, 8 ft. long, with gilt ends, 4/; or with coloured ends, 3/6 each.

ILLUMINATED TEXTS.

No. and Height.	ON CALICO.			ON PREPARED CLOTH.		
	Plainly Illuminated in Colours.	Richly Illuminated in Colours & Gold.	Outlined ready for Illumination	Plainly Illuminated in Colours.	Richly Illuminated in Colours & Gold.	Outlined ready for Illumination
680. 3 ft.	3/	4/	2/3	5/6	7/	4/
,, 5 ft.	4/6	5/6	3/6	8/	10/	5/6
,, 7 ft.	6/	7/6	4/6	10/6	12/6	7/
681. 6 ft.	6/	8/	4/6	10/6	13/	7/6
,, 9 ft.	8/	10/	6/	14/	17/	10/
,, 12 ft.	10/	12/6	7/6	17/6	21/	12/
682. 9 ft.	8/	10/	6/	14/	17/	10/
,, 12 ft.	10/	12/6	7/6	17/6	21/	12/
,, 15 ft.	12/	15/	9/	20/	24/	14/
,, 18 ft.	14/	17/6	10/6	23/	28/	16/6
683. 9 ft.	7/	9/	5/	13/	15/6	9/
,, 12 ft.	9/	11/	6/6	16/	19/	11/
,, 15 ft.	10/6	13/6	8/	18/	22/	13/
,, 18 ft.	12/	15/6	9/	20/	24/	14/6

The texts 680, 681, and 682 can be supplied plainly illuminated, without border, suitable for surrounding with evergreens, at the same price as quoted for "outlined ready for illumination."

PREPARED CLOTH OR CALICO,
WITH BORDER READY FOR AMATEURS TO FILL IN ANY TEXT REQUIRED.

ON PREPARED CALICO.

684.	Plainly illuminated,	.	.	.	.	1/4 per yard.
,,	Richly ,,					1/10 ,,
685.	Plainly ,,					1/6 ,,
,,	Richly ,,					2/ ,,
686.	Plainly ,,					2/ ,,
,,	Richly ,,					2/6 ,,

ON PREPARED CLOTH.

684.	Plainly illuminated,	.	.	.	.	2/6 per yard.
,,	Richly ,,					3/ ,,
685.	Plainly ,,					2/9 ,,
,,	Richly ,,					3/3 ,,
686.	Plainly ,,					3/3 ,,
,,	Richly ,,					3/9 ,,

If the lettering for texts is sketched ready for writing, Nos. 684 and 685 would be 9d., and No. 686, 1/ per yard extra.

Nos. 684 and 685 are 11 in. wide. No. 686 is 14 in. wide.

ILLUMINATED TEXTS.

No. and Height.	ON CALICO.			ON PREPARED CLOTH.		
	Plainly Illuminated in Colours.	Richly Illuminated in Colours & Gold.	Outlined. ready for Illumination	Plainly Illuminated in Colours.	Richly Illuminated in Colours & Gold.	Outlined ready for Illumination
687. 9 ft.	20/	25/	15/	33/	40/	21/
,, 12 ft.	25/	31/6	19/	38/	46/	25/
,, 15 ft.	30/	37/6	22/6	44/	54/	30/
,, 18 ft.	35/	44/	26/	50/	62/	35/
688. 9 ft.	24/	30/	18/	38/	46/	25/
,, 12 ft.	30/	37/	22/	47/	57/	30/
,, 15 ft.	36/	44/	26/	56/	68/	36/
,, 18 ft.	42/	50/	30/	64/	78/	42/
689. 9 ft.	18/	23/	13/	30/	37/	19/
,, 12 ft.	23/	28/6	17/	35/	43/	23/
,, 15 ft.	27/	34/	20/	40/	50/	27/
,, 18 ft.	31/	40/	23/	45/	57/	31/
690. 9 ft.	16/	20/	12/	28/	35/	16/
,, 12 ft.	20/	25/	15/	35/	42/	20/
,, 15 ft.	24/	30/	18/	40/	48/	24/
,, 18 ft.	28/	35/	21/	46/	56/	28/

No.		ON PREPARED CALICO.			ON PREPARED CLOTH.		
		Plainly Illuminated in Colours.	Richly Illuminated in Colours & Gold.	Outlined ready for Illumination.	Plainly Illuminated in Colours.	Richly Illuminated in Colours & Gold.	Outlined ready for Illumination.
691	2 feet	9/	12/0	5/6	13/	17/	9/
,,	3 feet	13/	16/6	7/	16/6	21/	10/
692	3 feet	8/6	10/6	6/	12/6	15/6	8/
,,	5 feet	12/6	15/6	8/	17/6	21/	12/
693	2 feet	5/	7/	3/	8/	10/6	4/6
,,	3 feet	7/6	10/6	4/6	12/	16/	6/6
694	per foot	1/2	1/6	/11	2/	2/6	1/4
695	per foot	/9	1/	/6	1/	1/6	/9
696	per foot	1/	1/3	/9	1/8	2/	1/2
697	per foot	1/	1/3	/9	1/8	2/	1/2
698	per foot	1/2	1/6	/11	2/	2/6	1/4
699	per foot	1/2	1/6	/11	2/	2/6	1/4
700	per foot	1/2	1/6	/11	2/	2/6	1/4
701	4 feet	4/6	6/6	3/6	8/	10/6	5/6
,,	6 feet	6/6	8/6	4/6	11/6	14/	7/6
702	7 feet	7/	9/	5/	12/	15/	8/6
,,	9 feet	8/	10/	6/	14/	17/	10/
,,	12 feet	10/	12/6	7/6	17/6	21/	11/6
703	9 feet	16/	20/	12/	28/	35/	18/
,,	12 feet	20/	25/	15/	35/	42/	22/
,,	15 feet	24/	30/	18/	40/	48/	26/
,,	18 feet	28/	35/	21/	46/	56/	30/
704	4 ft. × 3 ft.	15/6	18/6	9/	21/	24/	13/
,,	6 ft. × 4 ft.	20/	24/	12/	28/	32/	17/
705	4 ft. × 3 ft.	12/6	15/6	8/	17/6	21/	12/
,,	6 ft. × 4 ft.	17/	21/	10/6	24/6	28/	16/
706	per foot	1/2	1/6	/11	2/	2/6	1/4
707	per foot	1/2	1/6	/11	2/	2/6	1/4
708	5 feet	15/	22/	10/	21/	30/	14/
,,	7 feet	20/	29/	13/6	28/	40/	18/6
709	7 feet	13/6	19/	8/	19/	27/	12/6
,,	9 feet	18/	25/	11/6	25/	35/	16/6
,,	12 feet	24/	33/	15/6	33/	46/	22/
710	9 feet	9/	12/	7/6	15/	19/	11/6
,,	12 feet	11/	14/6	9/	18/6	23/	13/6
,,	15 feet	13/	17/	10/6	21/	26/	15/6
711	2 feet	15/	18/	8/	21/	25/	10/6
,,	3 feet	19/6	23/	10/	26/	30/	13/6
712	2 feet	16/	20/	9/	22/	28/	12/
,,	3 feet	21/	26/	11/6	27/	33/	15/
713	2 feet	15/	18/	8/	21/	25/	10/6
,,	3 feet	19/6	23/	10/	26/	30/	13/6
714	3 feet	21/	28/	14/	26/	35/	16/6
,,	5 feet	28/	37/	18/	35/	47/	22/
715	3 feet	25/	33/	16/6	31/6	42/	21/
,,	5 feet	34/	44/	22/	42/	56/	28/
716	3 feet	21/	28/	14/	26/	35/	16/6
,,	5 feet	28/	37/	18/	35/	47/	22/

The arch texts can be supplied plainly illuminated without border at the same price as quoted for "outlined ready for illumination." In ordering texts for arches of any of the designs except Nos. 698 and 706, it will be sufficient to give the size across the arch and its height, but to follow the curve of the arch the sizes should be given as shown on design No. 689, viz. A to B, B to C, and D to E. The latter gives the radius pretty accurately, but it is best to have a paper pattern taken and sent in addition to the above dimensions.

No.			ON PREPARED CALICO.			ON PREPARED CLOTH.		
			Plainly Illuminated in Colours.	Richly Illuminated in Colours & Gold.	Outlined ready for Illumination.	Plainly Illuminated in Colours.	Richly Illuminated in Colours & Gold.	Outlined ready for Illumination.
	ft.	in.						
717	1	6	8/	10/6	4/6	10/6	13/6	6/6
,,	2	0	10/	12/6	5/6	13/6	16/6	8/
718	1	6	10/	12/6	5/6	13/6	16/6	7/6
,,	2	0	12/6	15/6	7/	17/	20/	9/
719	1	6	8/	10/6	4/6	10/6	13/6	6/6
,,	2	0	10/	12/6	5/6	13/6	16/6	8/
720	3	0	13/	17/6	7/6	17/6	22/6	10/
,,	5	0	17/	22/	11/	24/	30/	14/
721	3	0	17/	22/	11/6	24/	30/	15/
,,	5	0	22/	30/	14/6	32/	40/	20/
722	3	0	13/	17/6	7/6	17/6	22/6	10/
,,	5	0	17/	24/	11/6	24/	30/	14/
723	2	0	10/6	14/	7/	15/	20/	9/6
,,	3	0	14/6	19/	8/6	21/	27/	12/
724	2	0	9/6	12/	6/	12/6	16/6	8/
,,	3	0	12/6	16/	8/	17/	21/	10/6
725	2	0	7/6	10/6	4/6	10/6	14/	7/
,,	3	0	10/	14/	6/	14/	19/	9/6
726	2	0	7/6	10/6	4/6	10/6	14/	7/6
,,	3	0	10/	14/	6/	14/	19/	9/6
727	2	0	9/6	12/	6/	12/6	16/6	8/
,,	3	0	12/6	16/	8/	17/	21/	10/6
728	2	0	9/	12/	6/	13/6	18/	8/6
,,	3	0	13/	17/	7/6	19/6	25/	10/
729	4	0	6/6	9/	4/6	10/	14/	7/
,,	6	0	9/6	13/6	6/6	15/	20/	10/
730	4	0	6/6	9/	4/6	10/	14/	7/
,,	6	0	9/6	13/6	6/6	15/	20/	10/

No.			ON PREPARED CALICO.			ON PREPARED CLOTH.		
			Plainly Illuminated in Colours.	Richly Illuminated in Colours & Gold.	Outlined ready for Illumination.	Plainly Illuminated in Colours.	Richly Illuminated in Colours & Gold.	Outlined Ready for Illumination.
731	Temporary	Reredos, 12 ft. long............	53/6	70/	35/	80/	105/	55/
,,	,,	Altar Frontal, 6 ft. long	20/	27/	12/	30/	40/	18/
732	,,	Reredos, 12 ft. long...	70/	90/	48/	105/	140/	75/
,,	,,	Altar Frontal, 6 ft. long.....	27/	36/	16/	40/	50/	22/
733	,,	Reredos, 12 ft. long..........	60/	80/	40/	90/	120/	65/
,,	,,	Altar Frontal, 6 ft. long	20/	27/	12/	30/	40/	18/
734	,,	Dossal, 6 ft. by 3 ft...........	22/	30/	13/6	33/	44/	20/
735	,,	,, ,, ,, ...	24/	33/	15/	36/	48/	22/
736	,,	,, ,, ,, ...	22/	30/	13/6	33/	44/	20/

Nos. 731 to 736 can be made to any sizes at proportionate prices.

737. Straw Tissue Letters, 2 in. high, 2/6 per dozen ; 3 in. high, 3/ per dozen.
  ,,   ,,   ,,   4 ,,   ,,   4/   ,,   5 ,,   ,,   5/   ,,

LETTERS AND DEVICES IN STRAW.

738. In high relief, 4 in., 10/6 per dozen ; 6 in., 14/ per dozen ; 8 in., 18/ per dozen.
  ,,   Flat   4 ,,   4/   6 ,,   5/   8 ,,   7/   ,,
739. In high relief, 12 ,, high, 10/ each ; 15 in. high, 12/6 each.
740.   ,,   ,,   10 ,, long, 6/ ,,   14 ,, long, 8/   ,,
741. Straw tissue,   9 ,, high, 2/6 ,,   12 ,, high, 3/   ,,
742. In high relief, 18 ,,   ,, 10/6 ,,   24 ,,   ,, 15/   ,,
743.   ,,   ,,   12 ,,   ,,   9/ ,,   15 ,,   ,, 12/   ,,
744.   ,,   ,,   12 ,,   ,,   8/6 ,,   15 ,,   ,, 11/6   ,,
745. Stars   4 ,,   ,,   1/ ,,   6 ,,   ,,   2/   ,,
  ,,   ,,   8 ,,   ,,   3/ ,,   12 ,,   ,,   6/   ,,

ZINC FLOWER-HOLDERS AND TROUGHS.

746. Zinc Hanging Flower-Holders, illuminated, large size, 8/ ; small size, 6/ each.
747. Basket   ,,   ,,   ,,   large size, 1/9 ; small size, 1/6 each.
748. Zinc   ,,   ,,   ,,   illuminated, 1/6 each ; plain painted, /9 each.
749. ,,   ,,   ,,   ,,   unpainted, 1/6 ; painted green, 2/6 ; or with gilt fleurs-de-lis, 6/ per dozen.
750. Wire Frame, with Zinc Flower Tubes, for Vases, 4/6 each.
751.   ,,   ,,   ,,   ,,   ,,   ,,   4/6   ,,
752. Zinc Flower-Holder for Vases, with springs, large size, 6/6 ; medium size, 5/ ; small size, 4/ each.
753. Cross, 1 ft. 4 in. long, 2/ each.
  ,, Upright Floating Cross on 3 steps, 1 ft. 6 in. high, 6/ ; 2 ft. high, 7/6 ; or decorated with flowers and moss, 18/ and 21/.
754. Zinc Flower Trough, 18 in. long, 6/ ; 24 in. long, 9/ ; 36 in. long, 15/.
754-A. Small size ditto,   12 ,,   ,,   2/.
755. Zinc Flower Trough, 18 ,,   ,,   2/6 ; 24 in. long, 4/ ; 36 in. long, 7/6.
756.   ,,   ,,   18 ,,   ,,   8/   24 ,, ,,   12/   36 ,,   ,,   20/.
757.   ,,   ,,   12 in. diameter, 6/ ; 15 in. diameter, 7/6 ; 18 in. diameter, 10/6.
758.   ,,   ,,   15 ,,   ,,   4/   18 ,,   ,,   5/   24 ,,   ,,   7/6.
759.   ,,   ,,   12 ,,   ,,   6/   15 ,,   ,,   7/6   18 ,,   ,,   10/6.
760. Illuminated Zinc Candle Shield, small size, 1/ ; large size, 1/6 each.
761.   ,,   ,,   ,,   ,,   ,,   1/   ,,   ,,   1/6
762. Zinc Altar Cross, with Water Troughs for Flowers, 16 in. high, 10/6 ; 24 in. high, 17/6.
763. Zinc Flower-Holder for Vase, with spring, 12 in. high, 6/6 ; 15 in. high, 9/.
764. Monogram Flower-Holder, 15 in. long, 9/.

FONT COVER FRAMES,
AS GROUNDWORK FOR DECORATIONS.

765. 4 ft. 6 in. high, 7/6 ; 6 ft. high, 10/6.
766. 3 ft. high, 14/ ; 4 ft. high, 18/.

POLISHED BRASS FLOWER VASES.

No.	ILLUMINATED.			PLAIN.		
	Height.	Height.	Height.	Height.	Height.	Height.
767.	5 in., 8/ ...	7½ in., 10/6 ...	9 in., 15/	5 in., 5/ ...	7½ in., 6/6 ...	9 in., 9/ each.
768.	8½ ,, 14/	...	...	8½ ,, 9/6 ...	...	,,
769.	5 ,, 9/ ...	7½ ,, 11/6 ...	9 ,, 16/	5 ,, 5/ ...	7½ ,, 6/6 ...	9 ,, 9/ ,,
770.	6 ,, 21/ ...	8 ,, 28/ ...	10 ,, 35/	6 ,, 16/6 ...	8 ,, 23/ ...	10 ,, 28/6 ,,
771.	4½ ,, 6/ ...	8 ,, 14/		4½ ,, 4/ ...	8 ,, 9/6 ...	,,
772.	10 ,, 36/	...	...	10 ,, 25/ ...	...	,,
773.	8 ,, 37/ ...	10 ,, 42/		8 ,, 32/ ...	10 ,, 36/ ...	,,
,,	,, without jewels, 8 in. 25/ ;	10 in., 30/		8 ,, 20/ ...	10 ,, 24/ ...	,,
774.	6 ,, 10/ ...	8 in. 13/6 ...	10 in., 16/6	6 ,, 7/6 ...	8 ,, 10/6 ...	10 ,, 13/6 ,,
775.	5½ ,, 10/6	...	...	5½ ,, 6/ ...	...	,,
776.	6 ,, 6/ ...	8 ,, 9/ ...	10 ,, 13/	6 ,, 4/6 ...	8 ,, 7/ ...	10 ,, 10/ ,,
777.	6 ,, 7/6 ...	8 ,, 11/		6 ,, 6/ ...	8 ,, 9/ ...	,,
778.	8 ,, 21/	...	...	...	...	,,
779.	6 ,, 18/ ...	8 ,, 23/ ...	10 ,, 28/	6 ,, 15/ ...	8 ,, 19/ ...	10 ,, 23/ ,,
780.	Ornament perforated,	...	...	8 ,, 10/6 ...	...	,,
781.	6 in., 23/ ...	8 in. 28/ ...	10 ,, 33/	6 in., 21 ...	8 ,, 25/ ...	10 ,, 30/ ,,
782.	9 ,, 30/	...	...	...	...	,,
784.	6 ,, 12/ ...	7½ ,, 16/ ...	9 ,, 21/	6 ,, 7/ ...	7½ ,, 10/ ...	9 ,, 13/6 ,,
785.	10 ,, 35/	...	...	10 ,, 28/ ...	...	,,
786.	6 ,, 9/6 ...	8 ,, 13/6 ...	10 ,, 18/	6 ,, 7/ ...	8 ,, 10/ ...	10 ,, 13/6 ,,

CHINA FLOWER VASES
ILLUMINATED IN COLOURS AND GOLD.

No.	Height.	Height.	Height.		
783.	6 in., 4/ ...	7½ in., 8/ ...	9 in., 12/ each.		
784.	5 ,, 4/ ...	6½ ,, 5/ ...	8 ,, 6/6 ,,		

ZINC FLOWER VASES.

776. 7 inches high, illuminated, 3/6 ; plain, 2/ each.

In deference to the wishes expressed by many of Messrs Cox & Sons' patrons, that some less expensive devices than those contained in previous editions of their Catalogue should be prepared, they have arranged a number of designs printed in outline, the colours of which can be filled in by hand, either by their own workmen, in which case they are considerably less expensive than when illuminated entirely by hand, or they can be supplied to Amateurs in outline for them to fill in the colours.

It will be understood that these designs are only printed in the sizes quoted. If wished of any other size, they would have to be drawn by hand.

The sizes given are those of the devices themselves, the cardboards would be larger.

Small Devices, 7 in. high, printed on Card, with the Colours and Gilding filled in by hand.

No.	Plainly Illuminated in Colours.	Richly Illuminated in Colours & Gold.	Outlined ready for Illumination.
788	1/4	2/	/8
789	1/6	2/6	/9
790	1/4	2/	/8
791	1/6	2/6	/9
792	1/4	2/	/8
793	1/6	2/6	/9
794	1/4	2/	/8
795	2/	3/	1/
796 to 803 } Cardboard Shields. 10½ in. by 7 in. each.	1/6	2/	/10
804 Pelican. 10 in. diameter,	4/6	6/	2/6
805 Agnus Dei, ,, ,,	4/6	6/	2/6
Printed Wall Devices.			
806 2 ft. diameter, . . .	7/6	10/6	4/
807 ,, ,, . . .	7/6	10/6	4/
808 2 ft. high, . . .	6/6	9/	3/
809 ,, ,, . . .	6/6	9/	3/
810 1 ft. 6 in. high, . . .	2/6	4/	1/3
811 ,, ,, . . .	2/6	4/	1/3
812 ,, ,, . . .	2/6	4/	1/3
813 ,, ,, . . .	2/6	4/	1/3
814 ,, ,, . . .	2/6	4/	1/3
815 ,, ,, . . .	2/6	4/	1/3
816 ,, ,, . . .	3/6	5/6	1/6
817 ,, ,, . . .	3/6	5/6	1/6
818 ,, ,, . . .	3/6	5/6	1/6
819 36 in. long, . . .	3/	4/	2/
820 36 in. by 36 in. . . .	7/6	10/6	5/
821 36 ,, by 24 ,, . . .	6/6	9/	4/
822 28 ,, by 19 ,, . . .	6/	8/6	3/
823 28 ,, by 19 ,, . . .	6/	8/6	3/
824 Rich illuminated, hand-painted text, 9 ft. long, on linen-backed cartoon paper, 18/.			

DOMESTIC CHRISTMAS DECORATIONS.

No.	ON CARDBOARD OR PREPARED CALICO.			ON PREPARED CLOTH.		
	Plainly Illuminated in Colours.	Richly Illuminated in Colours & Gold.	Outlined ready for Illumination.	Plainly Illuminated in Colours.	Richly Illuminated in Colours & Gold.	Outlined ready for Illumination.
825 6 ft. with Crown	16/	21/	12/	28/	35/	18/
826 or 827—						
3 ft.	7/	9/	4/6	11/	14/	7/6
5 ft.	9/6	11/6	6/6	15/6	19/	10/6
7 ft.	12/6	15/6	9/	20/	24/	13/6
828.—*As drawn, with Wreath Illuminated.*						
6 ft. long	16/	21/	12/	28/	35/	18/
9 ft. ,,	20/	25/	15/	35/	43/	22/
12 ft. ,,	25/	30/	18/6	43/	52/6	27/
829.—*Without Wreath.*						
6 ft. long	12/6	16/	10/	22/	28/	15/
9 ft. ,,	16/	20/	12/	28/	35/	18/
12 ft. ,,	20/	25/	15/	35/	42/	22/
829.—*Banner.*						
2 ft. 2 by 1 ft. 4	14/	17/	8/6	18/	21/	10/
3 ft. by 1 ft. 10	19/	22/	9/6	23/	27/	11/6
830.—*Banner.*						
2 ft. 2 by 1 ft. 4	10/6	12/6	6/6	13/6	16/	8/6
3 ft. by 1 ft. 10	14/	16/6	8/	18/	21/	10/6
831.—*Devices.*						
1 ft. 6 high	10/	12/6	6/6	13/6	16/6	8/6
2 ft. ,,	12/6	15/6	8/	17/	20/	10/6
3 ft. ,,	8/6	23/	11/6	25/	29/6	15/
832. 2 ft. high	12/6	15/6	8/	17/	20/	10/6
833.						
1 ft. 6 high	11/6	14/	7/	15/	18/	9/6
2 ft. ,,	14/	17/	9/	18/6	22/	11/
3 ft. ,,	20/	25/	13/	27/	31/6	16/6
834.—*Device as drawn, all Illuminated.*						
3 ft. long	14/	17/6	9/6	20/	23/6	12/6
5 ft. ,,	17/6	21/	11/6	25/	29/	16/
7 ft. ,,	21/	25/	13/6	30/	36/	20/
834.—*Scroll only, omitting Crown.*						
3 ft. long	7/6	9/	5/	11/	14/	7/6
5 ft. ,,	9/6	11/6	6/6	15/6	19/	10/6
7 ft. ,,	12/6	15/6	9/	20/	24/	13/6

835.—Chromo-Lithographed Motto, length, 5 ft. 6 in., price 5/, or in oak frame, 21/.

836.—Suggestion for forming Texts in Letters covered with Everlasting Flowers, for prices see plate 23.

MATERIALS FOR ILLUMINATING DECORATIONS.

Boxes of Colours, mixed and prepared for use, No. 1, 7/6; No. 2. 10/6.
  No. 1 contains 6 pots of colour, red, black, blue, white, green, and brown, 1 bottle of turpentine and 6 brushes.
  No. 2 contains in addition to the foregoing, 2 larger brushes, one bottle of gold size, one of liquid gold and one of liquid silver; or, if preferred, 2 books of gold leaf instead of the liquid gold and silver.
Pots of Colour prepared for use, Vermilion, 1/6; other colours, 1/ each.
Gold Size for applying leaf gold or bronze powder, /6 per bottle.
Gold Leaf. Best quality, 1/6 per book. Bronze Powder, /6 per packet.
Liquid Gold or Silver for Amateurs' use, either with quill pen or brush, in bottles, 1/ per bottle.
Crystal Frost, 1/ per packet, or 1/2 post free. This new material is used in a great variety of decorations. The best way of applying it to silk, paper, &c., is with a little clear liquid gum; but the smallest quantity of gum should be used, and the frost not applied till it is very nearly dry, just sticky.
Camel Hair Pencils.—Small sizes, 1/ per dozen; larger, 2/ per dozen; large camel hair brushes, for filling in colour, /6 each. *Sable Pencils.*—/6 and 1/ each.
Gilders' Kit.—For using leaf gold; consisting of cushion, knife, and brushes, 3/6.
Extra Stout Zinc.—Painted with four coats of colour, and prepared for decoration, 1/ per square foot. Zinc Tablets can be prepared to any size or shape required, and the writing and ornaments set out on them ready for Amateurs to illuminate.
Prepared Cloth.—3 ft. 6 ins. wide, painted ready for decoration, 4/6 per yard, or cut to any size, /6 per square foot.
Prepared Calico.—Superior quality, 37 ins. wide, 1/ per yard.

PLAIN AND COLOURED PAPER AND CARDBOARD.

Stout Cartoon Paper (white).—4 ft. 6 ins. wide, 1/ per yard. For texts, 10½ ins. wide, /3 per yard; 13¼ ins. wide, /4 per yard; 18 ins. wide, /5 per yard. If cut to special widths, the prices will be /1 per yard more.
Cartoon Paper, mounted on linen, 5 ft. wide, 4/6 per yard.
The "Cartoon paper" is very superior to "Lining paper" for decorative purposes.
Stout Lining Paper.—Width, 22 ins. 1/4 per piece; 30 ins. 2/ per piece.
Plain Cardboard, in sheets 24 by 20, 5/ per dozen; 30 by 22, 7/ per dozen; 26 by 26, 9/ per dozen.
Coloured Paper, good quality; crimson, 6/ per yard, 5/ per piece of twelve yards; blue, /6 per yard, 5/ per piece; black, /6 per yard, 5/ per piece. Inferior qualities can be supplied, but are not recommended for decorations.
Imitation Gold or Silver Paper, good quality, 1/ per sheet, 11/ per dozen sheets.
Flock Paper of good quality, plain, crimson, black, or green, without any pattern on it for backgrounds or cutting out, 1/ per yard, or 11/ per piece of 12 yards. Blue, 1/2 per yard, or 12/6 per piece.
Waterproof Paper (black).—/2 per yard; 1/9 per piece.
Straw Boards.—33 by 25, 6/ per dozen.

FABRICS, &c., FOR DECORATIONS.

Cotton Velvets, 22½ ins. wide, good quality, white, 3/6; other colours, 3/ per yard.
Cloth, 2 yards wide, suitable for decoration, crimson, 10/6 per yard; white or gold colour (superior quality), 18/ per yard.
Plain Cloth of Gold, cheap quality, 21 ins. wide, 7/6 per yard.
Rich Geometric Pattern Damask.—21 ins. wide, gold, 18/; silver, 14/6 per yard. Laces for trimmings, from /6 per yard.
White Long Cloth, superior quality, 1 yard wide, 1/ per yard.
Coloured Unglazed Cotton, specially made for decorations, 31 ins. wide, dark crimson, blue, or pink, 1/3 per yard; fine holland, 36 ins. wide, 1/1 per yard.
Worsted Binding.—Green or any other colour, 1/9 per dozen yards.
Worsted Cord, in any two colours, /4 per yard.
Tracing Braid, for outlining, gold or crimson and gold, 1/ per dozen yards.
White Cotton Wool, in sheets, best quality, /9; second quality, /6 per sheet.
Straw Tissue, /5 per sheet; 4/6 per dozen sheets. This tissue is very effective, and can be cut out easily to form letters, &c.
White Frosted Plush, for cutting out devices, texts, &c., very sparkling, 29 inches wide, 5/ per yard.
Plaited Straw, ⅛, ¼, ½, and ¾ inches wide, in bundles 1/ each.

EVERLASTING FLOWERS (*Gnaphaliums*).

The large and increasing demand for these flowers for church decorations enables Messrs Cox & Sons to supply them in the full-size bunches, about 8 or 9 ins. diameter, as received from abroad (not reduced in size, as is frequently done), at the following prices:—

	Per bunch.	Per doz. bunches.		Per bunch.	Per doz. bunches.
YELLOW	/10	9/	SOLFERINO	1/6	17/
WHITE	1/6	17/	ORANGE or LIGHT RED	1/	11/6
GREEN	1/	11/6	BLACK	1/6	17/
SPOTTED YELLOW	1/4	15/	BLUE	1/6	17/
CRIMSON	1/6	17/	VIOLET	1/6	17/
LILAC	1/6	17/	PURPLE	1/6	17/
PINK	1/6	17/	MAGENTA	1/6	17/

Mixed bunches, all colours, 1/8 per bunch.

A bunch of either of the above forwarded free by post on receipt of the price, with fourpence extra for postage. The everlasting flowers are sent in paper parcels, unless otherwise ordered. If wanted to be sent in a box (to avoid the risk of being crushed), 1/ for each dozen bunches, or a less number, to be added to the remittance.

The monotony produced by the use of evergreens only for wreaths, &c., is much relieved by the introduction of a few everlasting flowers.

LARGE EVERLASTING FLOWERS AND WREATHS.

HELICHRYSUMS.—Small bunches mixed, 6d. per bunch. Fine assorted colours, 4d. per dozen.

CAPE EVERLASTINGS.—These beautiful white dried flowers are sold for the benefit of Church work at Cape Town. When used, they should be warmed by steam, or in front of a fire, and opened out flat. The price is 4s. per hundred.

Wreaths of Immortelles, plain yellow, 1s. 6d., 2s., 2s. 6d., 3s. and 4s., according to size. These can also be supplied with inscriptions in black flowers, or any inscription wished can be added in metallic letters.

Wreaths of Immortelles, dried flowers and grasses, mixed, 6 in. diameter, 4s. ; 8 in. diameter, 6s. 6d. ; 10 in. diameter, 9s. each.

Bouquets of dried flowers and grasses for vases, 2s., 2s. 6d., and 5s. each.

IMITATION HOLLY BERRIES AND LEAVES, AND DRIED MOSS.

Imitation Holly Berries, 4d. per gross; 25 gross, 8s. ; 50 gross, 15s. A sample gross forwarded post free on receipt of six stamps.

Green Holly or Ivy Leaves, small size, 1s. per gross, or 10s. 6d. per dozen gross.
    ,,   ,,   large size, 1s. 6d. ,, ,, 16s. ,,

Variegated Holly Leaves, 2s. per gross, or 22s. per dozen gross.

Imitation Wreaths.—Wreaths one yard long made with the above leaves and berries, Green Holly or Ivy, 1s. each, or 11s. per dozen ; Variegated Holly, 1s. 6d. each, or 17s. per dozen. These Wreaths are fuller and contain many more leaves and berries than those ordinarily sold.

French Dried Moss, 6d. per packet, or 5s. per dozen packets.

IMITATION FLOWERS.

White paper roses, 2s. 6d. per dozen ; white paper camellias, 2s. 6d. per dozen.
Pink paper roses, 3s. per dozen ; pink paper camellias, 3s. per dozen.
Best Imitation Roses (*Linen*), White, 6s. per dozen ; Pink, 7s. per dozen.
  ,, with buds and leaves ,, 9s. ,,   ,, 10s. ,,
Best Imitation Camellias (*Linen*), White, 7s. per dozen ; Pink, 8s. per dozen.
  ,, with buds and leaves, ,, 10s. 6d. ,,   ,, 12s. ,,
Passion Flowers, of superior make, large size, 2s. 6d. each ; small size, 2s. each.
White Lilies ,, ,, natural size, 1s. 6d. each.
    ,,   ,, with buds and leaves, 2s. each.
Linen Daisies, large size, 1s. per dozen ; small size, 9d. per dozen.

Fresh Cut Flowers.—Messrs COX & SONS undertake commissions to procure these at the current market prices.

SUNDRIES.

	Per Bundle.		Per Bundle.
Stout Brass or Copper Wire,	. . 1s.	Stout Iron Wire, .	. . 6d.
Fine ,, ,,	. . 9d.	Fine ,, .	. . 4d.

Fine Wire, as used by artificial flower-makers, black, 6d. per reel ; green, 1s. per reel.

Perforated Zinc, 6d. per square foot : or cut in strips ½ inch wide, 3d. per yard ; or 1 inch wide, 5d. per yard.

Hoop Iron Clips, with a band of perforated zinc, can be supplied to fit any sized column, so as to avoid driving nails into the stone caps ; 1 foot diameter, or less, 1s. 6d. ; 1 foot 6 inches, 2s. ; 2 feet, 2s. 6d. ; 2 feet 6 inches, 3s. ; 3 feet, 3s. 6d.

Brass Pins, with steel points (similar to large drawing pins), for fastening up texts or devices, 7d. per dozen ; or 6s. 6d. per gross. Superior quality, 7s. 6d. per gross.

Fine Pointed Black Tacks, 4d. per packet. Copper Tacks, 9d. per packet.

Laths.—6 ft. long, 1 in. wide, 2s. per dozen ; 6 ft. long, 1½ ins. wide, 2s. 6d. per dozen. These laths will bend easily, and can be screwed together to form any length.

PROSPECTUS.

The business of the SOCIETY OF DECORATIVE ART, heretofore carried on at 25 Great Marlborough Street, has been transferred to Messrs COX & SONS, of Southampton Street, Strand, and College Wharf, Belvedere Road, Lambeth.

The working members of the Society, while its business was carried on in Marlborough Street, contributed a large number of original designs for Fittings, Decoration, Furniture, Upholstery, and numerous decorative accessories in Metal, Wood, and Stone. The whole of this extensive and valuable collection of drawings has been transferred to Messrs Cox & Sons, and is added to the large stock of designs which they are prepared to execute.

Mr S. J. Nicholl of Grove Road, St John's Wood, Architect, has consented to prepare new designs as they may be required, and also personally to devote attention to the execution of works during their progress. There will thus be an additional guarantee for the satisfactory workmanship and artistic character of the articles produced, as they will be subjected to the inspection of a gentleman who has devoted great attention to Domestic Gothic Art. Other professional gentlemen, who have made ancient Wood Work, Metal Work, and Stone Carving their special study, are in communication with Messrs Cox & Sons, and will be prepared to supply designs in the various departments of Decorative Art with which they are familiar.

In order to prevent a misapprehension as to the principle upon which the business is conducted, it is desirable to state that there is no intention to reproduce servile deceptive imitations of old works—or, in other words, to manufacture spurious *modern antiques*. The teaching of the old masters will be observed in the spirit rather than the letter. Educated people have learned to detest the heavy cumbrous forms and inharmonious colouring which were tolerated in the last and the earlier part of the present century; and it is not necessary that the reform should be conceived in a spirit of slavish adherence to mediæval models. Modern habits involve the use of a variety of convenient articles unknown in the Middle Ages, and domestic life has so much changed, that it would be childish affectation to require that modern art should literally copy that of feudal times. The study of Domestic Decoration, in order to be successful, must be undertaken in an eclectic spirit. We must respect the old models, not for their antiquity, but for their intrinsic excellence.

For many years past Messrs COX & SONS have manufactured Domestic Furniture of the best class, as well as Church Furniture, and the works they execute in continuation of the business of the Society of Decorative Art, are contained in the following enumeration :—

1. *Fittings.*   Joiners' Work, Staircases, Newels, Balusters, Dado-panelling, Parquetry Flooring, Chimney-pieces, Fireplaces, Gates, Railings, Balconies, Crestings, Finials, Lighting Arrangements, Coronæ, Standards, and Brackets to burn Gas, Oil, or Candles.

2. *Decorations.*   Wall Papers, Painted Decorations, Hand-painted Tiles, Stained Glass.

3. *Furniture.*   Sideboards, Book-cases, Cabinets, Tables, Chairs, Sofas, Pianoforte Cases, Wardrobes, Bedsteads, Washstands, and other Furniture and decorative accessories.

4. *Upholstery.*   Carpets, Curtains in Silk, Wool, and other Fabrics, Hand-painted Blinds, Table Covers, embroidered and plain, Table Linen.

5. *Sundries.*   Cabinet Ironmongery, Silver and Electro-plated Centre Pieces, Dessert and Flower Stands, Tea and Coffee Services, Inkstands, Clocks, Brackets, Frames, Fire-screens, Gothic Jewellery, and other ornamental fancy and useful sundries.

Extensive Show Rooms exclusively for Artistic Domestic Furniture and Decorative Accessories have been opened at 31 SOUTHAMPTON STREET.

An Illustrated Catalogue of Domestic Gothic Furniture, &c., forwarded on receipt of six postage stamps.

Mr JOHN KEITH, Silversmith to the Ecclesiological Society, is now associated with Messrs COX in their business as makers of Church Plate.

The extract from the Society of Arts' Report, given in another page, shows that Mr KEITH and Messrs COX have severally obtained medals of that Society for work exhibited in the Exhibition of 1871, some of which are shown in the above engraving.

Mr KEITH devotes the whole of his time to the superintendence of the manufacture of silver, plated, or electro-gilt goods, at the workshops, College Wharf, Belvedere Road, Lambeth, where his staff of skilled workmen is united with that of Messrs COX. He has relinquished the Manufacture of Church Plate at 59 Britannia Street, and 41 Westmoreland Place, City Road, London, and has ceased to supply Goods to Agents who have been hitherto authorised to represent him, and such Agencies are now discontinued.

From the year 1840, when Mr KEITH was appointed Church Plate Manufacturer to the Cambridge Camden Society, he worked under the directions of the Society until it discontinued to supply articles for Ecclesiastical purposes.

In the Great Exhibition of 1851 his Case of Plate, made from the designs and under the superintendence of W. BUTTERFIELD, ESQ., received the only Prize Medal given for Church Plate for the United Kingdom; and the same specimens received the First and Second Medals of the Goldsmiths' Company of London. In the Great Exhibition of 1862, Mr KEITH again received the only Medal awarded for similar Works of Art, executed from the designs of W. BUTTERFIELD, G. E. STREET, and W. BURGESS, Esqs.

An Illustrated Catalogue of Church Plate will be forwarded on application.

PUBLICATIONS BY COX & SONS.

ILLUSTRATED CATALOGUE OF CHURCH FURNITURE—With upwards of 800 Designs for Church Furniture, Gothic Metal Work, Decorations, Carpets, Hangings, Embroidery, &c., by eminent Church Architects and others. Price 6d., post free.

ILLUSTRATED CATALOGUE OF STAINED GLASS—New Edition. Containing 140 Designs, printed by Photo-lithography, and a List of nearly 150 Churches in which Stained Glass Windows, executed by them, have been placed. Price 6d., post free.

This Catalogue contains also full information as to the expense of windows in every variety and style, and such particulars with respect to the mode of measurement as will enable any one, in the first instance, to form a tolerably correct idea of the sum that will be required.

The Cartoons of the figures for Subject Windows executed by Messrs Cox & Sons, are prepared by an artist of eminence, who has devoted his life to the study of this branch of Art; and the greatly increased demand for windows painted from the Cartoons of this gentleman, is the best assurance Messrs Cox & Sons can have of the high appreciation of their stained glass.

ILLUSTRATED CATALOGUE OF MONUMENTS—With numerous Designs for Monuments, Tombs, Crosses, and Headstones in Granite, Marble, and Stone, Tomb-rails, Memorial Brasses, Mural Tablets, &c., by well-known Architects and others. Price 6d., post free.

New Editions of this Catalogue have from time to time been published, and the present one, which takes in its Illustrations the widest range—from the simple cross of wood, stone, or metal, to the most elaborate tomb in marble or polished granite—will, it is hoped, meet the requirements of the improved taste of the age.

ILLUSTRATED CATALOGUE OF DOMESTIC GOTHIC FURNITURE. Price 6d., post free.

The Judges appointed by the Society of Arts to report upon articles offered for the Great Exhibition of 1871, have awarded medals to Messrs Cox & Sons and their workmen for specimens of Silver Plate, Wrought-iron and Brass Work, Carved Stone and Wood Work, and Hand-painted Tile Decorations. The following extract from the Report of the Judges appears in the Journal of the Society for February 10, 1871:—

"Looking to the group of articles submitted by the firm alluded to, Messrs Cox & Sons, we would mention that it includes a number of specimens of Silversmiths' Work, in the shape of Church Plate, a polished brass Eagle Lectern (worked by J. Skelley), a large wrought-iron Gas Standard (well forged by W. Prendergast), a Font Cover of oak and brass, and a Panel for a Reredos, in hand-painted encaustic tiles. To the manufacturers we have awarded the Society's silver medal, accompanied with strong commendation of the well-directed and intelligent spirit of enterprise that has led to the mounting of a large establishment for the production of works of an artistic character. We have awarded a silver medal severally to Mr John Keith, under whose superintendence certain pieces of the silver work examined by us were produced, and to Mr B. J. Talbert, as designer of the chief works exhibited. We have further given money premiums to the two principal silversmiths employed.

"H. A. BOWLER.   RICHARD REDGRAVE.
GEORGE GODWIN.   M. DIGBY WYATT."

www.ingramcontent.com/pod-product-compliance
Lightning Source LLC
Chambersburg PA
CBHW030259170426
43202CB00009B/804